Israel

and the
Body of Christ

Don Hill

iUniverse, Inc.
Bloomington

ISRAEL AND THE BODY OF CHRIST

iUniverse books may be ordered through booksellers or by contacting:

iUniverse
1663 Liberty Drive
Bloomington, IN 47403
www.iuniverse.com
1-800-Authors (1-800-288-4677)

Because of the dynamic nature of the Internet, any web addresses or links contained in this book may have changed since publication and may no longer be valid. The views expressed in this work are solely those of the author and do not necessarily reflect the views of the publisher, and the publisher hereby disclaims any responsibility for them.

Unless otherwise indicated, Bible verses quoted in this book are from the New King James Version. Copyright © 1982 Thomas Nelson, Inc. Used by permission. All rights reserved.

Scripture quotations marked (NIV) are taken from THE HOLY BIBLE, NEW INTERNATIONAL VERSION®, NIV® Copyright © 1973, 1978, 1984, 2011 by Biblica, Inc.™ Used by permission. All rights reserved worldwide.

Scripture quotations marked (NLT) are taken from the Holy Bible, New Living Translation, copyright © 1996, 2004, 2007 by Tyndale House Foundation. Used by permission of Tyndale House Publishers, Inc., Carol Stream, Illinois 60188. All rights reserved.

Editing services by Karen Burkett of ChristianEditingServices.com.

Art and illustration by Teri Merrill
Web site www.artbyteri.net

Author – Don Hill - jdhill42@gmail.com

ISBN: 978-1-4620-3567-0 (sc)
ISBN: 978-1-4620-3569-4 (hc)
ISBN: 978-1-4620-3568-7 (e)

Printed in the United States of America.

iUniverse rev. date: 5/3/2013

Contents

Acknowledgments

I acknowledge and thank God for giving me the thoughts and helping me stay focused as I wrote this book. I pray its words will bring glory to Him. I depend on His help in all things and desire to draw as close to Him as I can.

I sincerely thank these people who helped me through this journey . . .

- Chris Kinata came to my aid with editing and research as I started.
- My brother, Edwin Hill, helped with Bible research.
- My granddaughter, Delynn Warren, who taught English and Spanish, contributed her editing skills.
- My daughter, Carol Moe, continued to give support with editing and research from start to finish.
- Ann Alderson, during her proofreading, asked many questions that sent me back to the Bible in order to explain what I was trying to say.
- Teri Merrill provided art and illustration for the front cover. Her web site is www.artbyteri.net.
- God blessed me when I found Karen Burkett of

Christian Editing Services. She used *The Christians Writer's Manual of Style* as a guideline. She has a great understanding of the Bible, and we could discuss my writing from a biblical perspective and stay on focus with a smooth flow.

Preface

I am passionate about understanding God's Word through prayer, Bible study, research, and Bible conferences. With God's help, I have learned exciting truths and gained new insights through these concentrated studies of His Word. And now God has nudged me—and given me the courage—to write what I have learned.

I hope as you read this book, you will be inspired to study the Word with new fervor as you recognize the urgency of the times in which we live. We will look at significant prophecies being fulfilled all around us—none more important than the renewed anguish the Israelis are experiencing.

Have you ever looked at the size of Israel on a world globe? So small, and yet consistently the center of world focus. In this book, we will look at how the biblical words written so many years ago relate to Israel and the Body of Christ today. We will examine often overlooked or misunderstood passages, opening new avenues of discovery.

I pray that as we take this journey of discovery together, you will be as blessed as I have been with new understanding of God's message and how it relates to each of us today. I pray these truths will energize you and fill you with a passion to share them with others. I pray you will be like Peter and John when they said, "As for us, we cannot help speaking about what we have seen and heard" (Acts 4:20 NIV).

Tradition—or Truth?

I have read the Bible for most of my life and used to think my scriptural knowledge was reasonably solid. But as I began to dig deeper, I found much of what I thought I knew was based on tradition, not Scripture. Or I had gone astray by reading isolated scriptures without understanding the context. Sometimes my lack of understanding of Jewish culture led me to error.

The story of the wise men who visited baby Jesus is just one example of the way tradition influences us. Christmas cards and church dramas portray three men visiting a barn with animals and hay in the background. However, we have no proof there were only *three* wise men. And they did not visit the manger. They traveled over a year to get to Bethlehem from Persia. By the time they arrived, Joseph, Mary, and Jesus were living in a house.

There could have been up to three hundred wise men coming from other places at various times, which certainly would have gained Herod's attention. He asked the wise men when they had first seen the star and learned from their response that the King of the Jews would be under two years old (Matthew 2:2). He then ordered the slaughter of all male children in the surrounding area who were younger than two.

Throughout this book, I will share many examples of truth replacing my traditional thinking as I grew in my understanding of God's Word.

The Bible: Who Is the Intended Audience?

Many people misunderstand who the intended recipient of the Bible was. While writing this book, I discussed this topic with many church leaders, including preachers and seminary students. I found the majority do not understand that Jesus came to fulfill the covenants and the law, God's promises to Israel.

> But Peter, standing up with the eleven, raised his voice and said to them, "Men of Judea and all who dwell in Jerusalem, let this be known to you, and heed my word." (Acts 2:14)

> "Men of Israel, hear these words." (Acts 2:22)

> "The God of Abraham, Isaac, and Jacob, the God of our fathers . . ." (Acts 3:13)

Peter was talking to the Jews of Judea living in Jerusalem—"men of Israel," the "God of Abraham," and "God of our father." He was preaching to the Jews, not the Gentiles.

> Now those who were scattered after the persecution that arose over Stephen traveled as far as Phoenicia, Cyprus, and Antioch, preaching the word to no one but the Jews only. (Acts 11:19)

To whom were the scattered Jewish believers preaching? Only Jews. That is from the Scripture, not me.

The next verse shows that during Jesus' ministry, He kept the law.

> "See that you tell no one; but go your way, show yourself to the priest, and offer the gift that Moses commanded, as a testimony to them." (Jesus' words in Matthew 8:4)

Jesus kept the law, and He ministered to Israel. Read what He said:

> But He answered and said, "I was not sent except to the lost sheep of the house of Israel." (Matthew 15:24)

Scriptures mentioning the house of Israel and the Jews mean more when we understand what God wanted us to know from His Word. In the next verse, Peter was talking to the Jews but added a message to both Jews and Gentiles.

> "You are sons of the prophets, and of the covenant which God made with our fathers, saying to Abraham, *'And in your seed all the families of the earth shall be blessed.'*" (Acts 3:25)

Peter is talking to the sons of the prophets, Israel, the Jews. The covenant was with them, not the Gentiles. God covenanted with Abraham. Jesus confirmed the promise to Israel, and He will keep that promise.

In the last part of the verse, Peter is letting us know both

Jews and Gentiles will be blessed through Abraham's seed, Jesus Christ.

Prophecy Fulfilled: How Many Times?

Much of my studying has focused on biblical prophecy. Prophecies given, prophecies fulfilled. When I learned how God has already fulfilled so many prophecies—down to the last detail—I became more eager to study prophecies He has not yet fulfilled. I developed a sense of anticipation for what is to come.

Scriptures explaining how God has worked in the past and is working now give us more understanding about the future. Knowing more about the future will make us feel more secure with the present.

Have you ever read a prophecy and wondered whether it was fulfilled by some event in the past or is meant for the future? The answer could be *both*. Some Bible prophecies are fulfilled more than once. Some have already been fulfilled but will be fulfilled again in the future. For example, in Matthew 24:15, Jesus referred to the *"abomination of desolation, spoken of by Daniel the prophet."* (The *abomination of desolation* means "the abomination makes it desolate.")

> "Then he shall confirm a covenant with many for one week; But in the middle of the week He shall bring an end to sacrifice and offering. And on the wing of abominations shall be one who makes desolate, Even until the consummation, which is determined, is poured out on the desolate." (Daniel 9:27)

> "And forces shall be mustered by him, and they shall defile the sanctuary fortress; then they shall take away the daily *sacrifices,* and place *there* the abomination of desolation." (Daniel 11:31)

We learn from books by Josephus and other Bible scholars that Antiochus, a Syrian king, occupied Jerusalem in 168 BC and polluted the temple by offering a hog and erecting an idol to Zeus. Definitely an abomination of desolation. We know that in AD 70 Titus destroyed the temple and set up an idol to mock the Jews. A second fulfillment of prophecy about the abomination of desolation. A third is yet to come: Scholars believe Daniel 9:27 refers to the Antichrist, who will commit an abomination of desolation against God midway through the Great Tribulation.

Another example of prophecies being fulfilled more than once involves prophecies about the coming of Christ. Ancient readers studying the Old Testament should have discovered there were to be two events concerning the Messiah: (1) Christ's birth, life, death on the cross, and resurrection; (2) Christ's second coming to rule on earth during the millennium. These are two distinct events. The suffering of Christ, who substituted His life on the cross for our sins and gave us life in Him, has happened. His second coming is still in the future. By studying the Bible, we can see how many prophecies were fulfilled by the first event. And we can see prophecies about what will happen before His second coming fulfilled in the past and being fulfilled now. Those prophecies include many types of events: wars, natural disasters, moral decline, and more. Most of them center on

Israel and God's chosen people—the Jews. Believers waiting for the second event can take comfort in knowing Jesus is coming back—and they will spend eternity with Him.

The book of Revelation is a revelation of Jesus Christ. Many Old Testament prophecies about the Great Tribulation and Jesus' return are woven throughout the book.

Peter reminds us of similar prophecies about the Great Tribulation that have not yet been fulfilled. In Acts 2:16–24, Peter was preaching to the men of Judea and quoted from the prophet Joel. Part of Joel's prophecy has been fulfilled. Part of it is yet to be fulfilled.

> *And it shall come to pass in the last days, says God, That*
> *I will pour out of My Spirit on all flesh.* (Acts 2:17)

Joel prophesied that the Spirit would come; Jesus fulfilled that promise when He sent the Spirit (John14:16). "All flesh" includes both Jews and Gentiles in one Body of Christ. Both Jews and Gentiles have (and will) experienced the outpouring of the Spirit and ministries done through His power.

The second part of Joel's prophecy quoted by Peter has not yet been fulfilled.

> *I will show wonders in heaven above And signs in the*
> *earth beneath: Blood and fire and vapor of smoke.* (Acts
> 2:19)

The heavenly wonders refer to the end of this age, that awesome day of the LORD also referred to as the Great Tribulation. Blood and fire correspond with Revelation

8:7–9. Revelation 6:12 describes the "great earthquake" and blood. Revelation 9:18 and other Bible passages mention the fire and smoke.

A study of prophecy shows just how real God is—only in the Bible do we find prophecies given hundreds and even thousands of years before events occurred that have been fulfilled in detail exactly as the prophet said. Understanding this can give us confidence that we will see all the unfulfilled prophecies come to pass. It can help us understand the chaos around us and give us hope.

Reading and studying the Bible is essential for growth in God, but book knowledge is not enough. We need to understand what these truths mean to us personally. Many avoid reading the book of Revelation because they think it is too frightening or too difficult to understand. I believe it is best to interpret its chapters literally, as the Bible indicates many of its symbols have a literal meaning. If we want to know Christ better and have a better understanding of the world today and what is to come, we need to prayerfully examine this all-important book of the Bible. The unknown can be frightening. As believers, once we understand the great future Christ has for us, we can enjoy Him more because we know our future is secure in Him.

†

We live in a crucial time of great change. Morality is decaying before our eyes. Christians lack the boldness to stand against what is happening. Many Christians and non-Christians have relaxed their values and are comfortable listening to a preacher give a feel-good message that has nothing to do with the authentic good news of salvation by grace through faith in Jesus Christ. Many Christians in this country are turning their hearts away from God's virtues and morals as they allow their freedom in God to be pushed aside.

Jesus came to earth the first time as a servant who died and rose from the dead so we may have life through Him. He is coming back as King, at which time He will pour out His wrath on His enemies.

As I watch so many prophecies being fulfilled, I have to believe Jesus will not tarry much longer, so get ready for the ride of your life. Jesus Christ will come back. Are you ready? Everlasting darkness awaits those who reject Him. The Bible tells us the end of the story and the wondrous future that awaits those who trust in Him.

How will this book benefit you? You will gain understanding about . . .

- The Abrahamic covenant.
- The importance of Genesis to us today.
- The importance of understanding the Old Testament to accurately interpret the New Testament.
- The two distinct plans God has for Israel and for the Gentiles. Salvation is for everyone who believes—both Jew and Gentile, but when it comes to the land of Israel, the plans are different for Jews and Gentiles. The two are never used interchangeably.
- The false teaching of Replacement Theology that comes from not interpreting the Scriptures correctly.

- Misunderstandings of some scriptures in the four Gospels about how Jesus came to fulfill the Law.
- Religions and apostasy. How the world is pushing God aside and how easy it is to be deceived by false teaching.
- The church—past, present, and future.
- Israel and biblical prophecy being fulfilled today.
- The animosity between the Muslims and the Jews.
- What can we expect?
- Our Redeemer. Will you be ready?

chapter 1

God's Covenant with Abraham

Now the LORD had said to Abram: "Get out of your country, from your family And from your father's house, To a land that I will show you. I will make you a great nation; I will bless you And make your name great; And you shall be a blessing. I will bless those who bless you, And I will curse him who curses you; And in you all the families of the earth shall be blessed." (Genesis 12:1–3)

†

Throughout history, God has dealt with Israel and the church as two distinct groups. Without understanding that, we can easily err by thinking Israel and the church are the same. This misconception will prevent us from correctly understanding Scripture.

Understanding God's covenant with Abraham lays a sound foundation for making sense of Scripture—and all of history since then. This understanding will also help us better interpret current events and the last days yet to come (and possibly very near).

We can read about God's covenant with Abraham in Genesis—a covenant that set the stage for all of God's promises to Israel that followed. The covenant—and the entire Bible—points to Jesus Christ. Understanding this enables us to grasp what Jesus meant when He said He came to fulfill the law. We will understand how God sees the Body of Christ, His church. And we will see that although He has blessed the Gentiles for almost two thousand years, God is still working with Israel. Understanding the covenant brings insight into God's plan and will influence our worldview and how we live.

Terminology

Clarifying certain terms will help us better grasp the meaning and impact of God's covenant with Abraham.

Scripture refers to Israel as God's chosen people: Abraham was the father of the Jews—his son, Isaac's son Jacob, and Jacob's descendants. God changed Jacob's name to Israel. I believe this was the start of the Jewish race.

The terms *church of God* and *body of the church* can sometimes be used interchangeably. The *Body of Christ* (Ephesians 4:12) identifies believers who have accepted Christ in this age of grace.

The Old Testament believers and the Body of Christ are separate groups but both are part of the kingdom of God. *The kingdom of God* is sometimes referred to as *the kingdom of heaven*. Examples are found in Matthew 3:2 and other scriptures throughout the New Testament. Jesus is in heaven and the kingdom is in heaven. When Jesus returns to earth, the kingdom will be on earth.

The word *dispensation,* often used in Scripture, has several meanings. Notes in the original Scofield Reference Bible read, "A dispensation is a period of time during which man is tested in respect of obedience to specific revelation of the will of God."

God gave Moses the Law at Mount Sinai (Leviticus 27:34), and Moses dispensed the Law to God's people. These acts could be considered the dispensation of law. Scripture refers to today's church (believers in Christ) as the Body of Christ.

After Paul was saved and God chose him to be the apostle to the Gentiles, he did not immediately go to Jerusalem but rather to Arabia (Galatians 1:17).

> For I neither received it from man, nor was I taught *it,* but *it came* through the revelation of Jesus Christ. (Galatians 1:12)

Paul received the truth of the gospel, a mystery (secret) that formerly had not been revealed; he dispensed the doctrines of grace.

> That in the dispensation of the fullness of the times He might gather together in one all things in Christ, both which are in heaven and which are on earth—in Him. (Ephesians 1:10)

Spiritually speaking, there are three groups of people: The first is the Old Testament believers. The second is the Body of Christ, which includes Jews and Gentiles who have received Christ as their Lord and Savior. The third group consists of nonbelievers who have not accepted Jesus Christ as their personal Savior.

Think of a large box and three big balls. One ball, labeled "Israel," includes Old Testament believers before and after Abraham, up until Pentecost. Another ball, labeled "Body of Christ" consists of believers from the time the church was started until the present day. These two balls are inside the box labeled "Kingdom of God." The other ball is labeled "nonbelievers"—Old Testament and church age nonbelievers. That ball is outside the box. Those groups of people are not part of the kingdom of God.

†

God's Covenant with Abraham

Webster's defines *covenant* as "a formal, solemn, and binding agreement." Many nations and people use covenants—man to man, individual to group, and nation to nation.

In Abraham's time, a covenant was normally made by slaughtering animals, cutting them into pieces, and placing the meat pieces opposite the people involved. Participants would then walk between the meat pieces. This would bind the covenant for each person taking part. If a person broke the covenant, that person would be required to pour out his blood (give his life) as a forfeit for the animals that poured out their blood for the covenant. In most covenants, both parties would participate in the blood sacrifice. Abraham would have been familiar with this procedure.

In the verses below, we see that God had already brought Abram (his name before it was changed to Abraham in Genesis 17:5) out of Ur and given him the land listed at the end of the passage. Numbers 34:1–12 describes the land God gave to His chosen people.

> Then He said to him, "I *am* the LORD, who brought you out of Ur of the Chaldeans, to give you this land to inherit it." And he said, "Lord God, how shall I know that I will inherit it?"
>
> So He said to him, "Bring Me a three-year-old heifer, a three-year-old female goat, a three-year-old ram, a turtledove, and a young pigeon." Then he brought all these to Him and cut them in two, down the middle, and placed each piece opposite the other; but he did not cut the birds in two. And when the vultures came down on the carcasses, Abram drove them away. Now when the sun was going down, a deep sleep fell upon Abram; and behold, horror *and* great darkness fell upon him. Then He said to Abram: "Know certainly that your descendants will be strangers in a land *that is* not theirs, and will serve them, and they will afflict them four hundred years. And also the nation whom they serve I will judge; afterward they shall come out with great possessions. Now as for you, you shall go to your fathers in peace; you shall be buried at a good old age. But in the fourth generation they shall return here, for the iniquity of the Amorites *is* not yet complete." And it came to pass, when the sun went down and it was dark, that behold, there appeared a smoking oven and a burning torch that passed

> between those pieces. On the same day the LORD
> made a covenant with Abram, saying: "To your
> descendants I have given this land, from the river
> of Egypt to the great river, the River Euphrates—
> the Kenites, the Kenezzites, the Kadmonites,
> the Hittites, the Perizzites, the Rephaim, the
> Amorites, the Canaanites, the Girgashites, and
> the Jebusites." (Genesis 15:7-21)

Only the "burning torch . . . passed between those pieces." This was a promise from God. Abram did not participate in the covenant. He could do nothing to break it. God confirmed this covenant with Isaac and Jacob. It will be completed in full when Jesus comes back to set up His kingdom on earth.

God assured Abram he would have a good life and live to an old age, but his descendants would not do as well.

> Then He said to Abram: "Know certainly that
> your descendants will be strangers in a land *that*
> is not theirs, and will serve them, and they will
> afflict them four hundred years." (Genesis 15:13)

That prophecy was fulfilled to the very day. God sent Moses to lead His people out of captivity in Egypt. The first generations, however, were punished for not believing God would protect them. All adults who walked out of Egypt— except Joshua and Caleb—died sometime during the forty years the Hebrews wandered in the wilderness. Joshua and Caleb had faith and believed God. Later, Joshua led God's people into the Promised Land.

Unconditional

The New Testament book of Hebrews confirms the divine nature of the covenant with Abraham:

> For when God made a promise to Abraham, because He could swear by no one greater, He swore by Himself. (Hebrews 6:13)

The covenant was made only to Israel and will be fulfilled with Israel. It is eternal. Although many people disagree, we know from Scripture that it is unconditional. It is permanent. The final fulfillment is a future event that will occur only when Christ comes back to complete the covenant.

Many people today do not believe the covenant was unconditional. However, all scriptural evidence confirms that it was. J. Dwight Pentecost writes the following in his book *Things to Come*:

> (2) Except for the original condition of leaving his homeland and going to the Promised Land, the covenant is made with no conditions whatever . . .

> (3) The Abrahamic Covenant is confirmed repeatedly by reiteration and enlargement. In none of these instances are any of the added promises conditioned upon the faithfulness of Abraham's seed or of Abraham himself. . . . Nothing is said about it being conditioned upon the future faithfulness of either Abraham or his seed.[1]

This covenant was confirmed by God. God told Abraham

to get out of the country, which he did. In Genesis 12:2, God stated He would make him a great nation, which He did.

The covenant was affirmed again in 2 Samuel 7:10. Here God sent the prophet Nathan to David to tell him about a time in the future when He would provide a place for Israel to call its own, a time when it would not be oppressed by others. This has not yet happened, but it will.

The Seed of Israel

It is important to establish the meaning of *the seed of Israel*. Battles are being fought constantly today because of disagreements about Israel's land and misunderstandings about the seed of Abraham.

Abram and Sarai (their names before being changed to Abraham and Sarah) were getting up in years but had not yet seen the heir God had promised. Sarai was getting impatient and suggested to Abram that he have a child by Hagar, her Egyptian maidservant (see Genesis 16:1–3). Abram listened to her and had a son (Ishmael) with Hagar. Ishmael was Abram's firstborn son.

> God changed Abram's name to Abraham and told him, "I have made you a father of many nations." (Genesis 17:5)

Abram *was* eighty-six years old when Ishmael was born (Genesis 16:15). God then changed Sarai's name to Sarah (Genesis 17:15). In verses 16 and 17, He told Abraham that Sarah would have a son:

"I will bless her and also give you a son by her;
then I will bless her, and she shall be *a mother
of* nations; kings of peoples shall be from her."
(Genesis 17:16)

Abraham loved Ishmael and was concerned about him.
He pleaded with God: "Oh, that Ishmael might live before
You!" (Genesis 17:18).

Then God said: "No, Sarah your wife shall bear
you a son, and you shall call his name Isaac; I will
establish My covenant with him for an everlasting
covenant, *and* with his descendants after him."
(Genesis 17:19)

God made it clear the everlasting covenant was with the
son Abraham and Sarah would have. However, in Genesis
17:20 God assured Abraham He had blessed Ishmael.
"Behold, I have blessed him, and will make him fruitful,
and will multiply him exceedingly. He shall beget twelve
princes, and I will make him a great nation."

Ishmael was blessed and his descendants (living
predominately in the Middle East) have been blessed. Look
at all the oil and the wealth in the Middle East. God made
it clear, however, that Ishmael was not the physical seed to
carry through the covenant. The covenant would continue
through the son Sarah would bear (Isaac). And many years
later, through the line of Isaac's descendants, would come
Jesus Christ, the promised Messiah. Abraham was one
hundred and Sarah was ninety when Isaac was born.

"My covenant I will establish with Isaac, whom

> Sarah shall bear to you at this set time next year."
> (Genesis 17:21)

God later confirmed this covenant through Moses (Deuteronomy 1:7-8).

Scriptures throughout the Bible refer to Abraham, Isaac, and Jacob. Jacob was the physical seed of Isaac. God later changed Jacob's name to Israel (Genesis 32:28), referring to their physical lineage. The term *Israel* literally means "the physical descendant of Abraham."

While Esau and Jacob were in their mother's womb, their mother Rebekah—Isaac's wife—asked the LORD about the struggle in her womb.

> And the LORD said to her: "Two nations *are* in your womb, Two peoples shall be separated from your body; *One* people shall be stronger than the other, And the older shall serve the younger."
> (Genesis 25:23)

Before they were born, God had planned that Esau and Isaac's descendants would each lead a nation. Many Muslims think they should be entitled to the Promised Land. After all, Ishmael was Abraham's first son, and in Genesis 21:18, God told Hagar He would make her son "a great nation." In the next generation, Esau and Jacob were twins, but since Esau was born first, many today believe Esau should have been Isaac's chosen since he was older than Jacob. (See Genesis 25:29-34 where it speaks about Esau's birthright.) In verse 32, we read that Esau did not have faith nor value his birthright. However, Muslims insist that Esau—being Isaac's firstborn—should be favored.

Before God chose Abraham, all the people on earth were Gentiles. Abraham was a Gentile. (When I use the word *Gentile* in this text, it encompasses everybody but the Jews.) Abraham is called the father of the Jewish race, but he was not a Jew. Abraham's seed continued to Isaac, then to Jacob, whose name God changed to Israel.

Although Esau was the firstborn, God chose Jacob before they came out of their mother's womb as He had already established that the "older shall serve the younger." God was illustrating that the covenant was selective, and He would fulfill it with whomever He wanted. Some people try to put God in a box. However, His ways are not our ways, and He does things we do not understand.

There are many scriptures about God's chosen people. He often calls them "My people." His covenant is with Israel, and only He can break it. Even when Abraham sinned after the covenant was made, God confirmed the covenant with Isaac and Jacob.

The covenant is just as fresh and real today as the day God made it. Scripture talks about an everlasting covenant (Genesis 17). This covenant was made before the promise between God and Abraham in which God had Abraham circumcise every male child on the eighth day.

The Abrahamic covenant promises are to Israel—descendants of Abraham, Isaac, and Jacob—and the land belongs to them. In the future, that land will be theirs. God also promises Israel an everlasting existence as a nation. Israel was recognized as a nation in May 1948; however, the Jewish people do not yet have permanent possession of all the land God promised to Abraham. This is yet to be fulfilled—but it will happen.

Physical Seed and Spiritual Seed

If the promise and covenant are made to Israel, where does the church fit in?

The New Testament distinguishes between Israel and the church and between the Jews and Gentiles. Luke 7:5 and 21:10 refer to Israel as a nation. The church is not a nation and never will be. In Romans 11, Paul is talking to the Jews and explaining the difference between them and Gentiles. In verse 25, he talks about Israel as one and the Gentiles as separate. In 1 Corinthians 10:32, Paul refers to "the Jews" and "the church of God"—two separate entities. You can find this difference throughout the New Testament. We can clearly conclude from these scriptures that Israel is set apart from the church: Israel is a nation. The Body of Christ is not.

We have discussed the physical descendants of Abraham who formed the nation of Israel. This is Abraham's physical seed. But the Scriptures also mention the spiritual seed of Abraham. The spiritual seed includes everyone—both Jew and Gentile—who has received Jesus Christ as Savior. All who go into the millennium will be the spiritual seed of Abraham. This group will include Gentiles who have received Jesus Christ as Lord and Savior and Jews who have accepted Yeshua (the Hebrew word for Jesus) as their Savior and Messiah.

> Therefore know that *only* those who are of faith
> are sons of Abraham. (Galatians 3:7)

This verse is so easy to take out of context. It is saying that Abraham's faith in God (Genesis 15:6) is the same saving faith we have as believers.

These words from Genesis 13 describe physical seed descending from Abraham, Isaac, and Jacob:

> "And I make your descendants as the dust of the earth; so that if a man could number the dust of the earth, *then* your descendants also could be numbered." (Genesis 13:16)

Now go over two chapters to Genesis 15.

> Then He brought him outside and said, "Look now toward heaven, and count the stars if you are able to number them." And He said to him, "So shall your descendants be." (Genesis 15:5)

> And he believed in the LORD, and He accounted it to him for righteousness. (Genesis 15:6)

These words describe Abraham's spiritual seed—all believers, both Jew and Gentile. The word *believed* was first used in Genesis 15:6.

> So then those who *are* of faith are blessed with believing Abraham. (Galatians 3:9)

This is a promise of salvation to everybody who believes. Both Jews and Gentiles come to God through the spiritual seed. All believers in Christ are spiritual children of Abraham. We are Abraham's seed and heirs according to the promise.

> And if you *are* Christ's, then you are Abraham's seed, and heirs according to the promise. (Galatians 3:29)

All nations will be blessed through Abraham's spiritual seed. Through Christ, we are heirs because we are in Christ.

The spiritual blessing is for all believers, but the physical seed of Abraham will come from the line of Isaac, Jacob, and their descendants. All believers will receive the promises of God. (For more references on the seed of Abraham, see the following scriptures: Genesis 21:12; 26:24; 28:4; 28:13; Exodus 32:13; 33:1; Joshua 24:3; 2 Chronicles 20:7; Psalm 105:6; Isaiah 41:8; Jeremiah 33:26; Acts 3:25; Romans 4:13; 9:7; 11:1; 2 Corinthians 11:22; Galatians 3:16; Hebrews 2:16.)

Obadiah's Prophecy

Before closing this chapter, I will share from the prophet Obadiah, who wrote around 840 BC. The prophetic book of Obadiah has only one chapter with twenty-one verses. He talks about God's chosen people, Israel, and how He will care for them and execute judgment against those who oppose them. This is prophecy that will happen in the end times, which may be near.

> For the day of the LORD upon all the nations

is near; As you have done, it shall be done to you; Your reprisal shall return upon your head. (Obadiah 1:15)

The prophet Obadiah condemned the Edomites—descendants of Esau, Jacob's twin brother—for their refusal to aid Israel during the wilderness wandering (Numbers 20:14–21). Obadiah is also talking about the end time. In verse 15, "for the day of the LORD" speaks of the Great Tribulation, a seven-year period that culminates when Jesus Christ physically comes back to earth.

God will punish those who wrong and persecute Israel. Notice the same verse of Obadiah speaks of "all the nations." The Bible says what it means and means what it says. If the United States spends more time aiding and flattering the enemies of Israel than supporting and being a friend to Israel, we can expect the warning "Your reprisal shall return upon your head" to apply to our country, and we will suffer the consequences.

We read about Israel's final conquest in verse 18: "And no survivor shall *remain* of the house of Esau."

Then saviors shall come to Mount Zion To judge the mountains of Esau, And the kingdom shall be the LORD's. (Obadiah 1:21)

As we grow in our understanding of the Abrahamic covenant and God's chosen people, our desire to support Israel should grow (Genesis 12:3; Zechariah 12:9–14:12).

chapter 2

Replacement Theology

Some people claim Israel is no longer God's chosen people and God has canceled all plans for that nation. Replacement Theology says the church has replaced Israel in God's plan. This idea has been around since AD 160 and comes from a misunderstanding of the Abrahamic covenant. The word *supersession* has also been used to say the church supersedes or takes precedence over Israel.

Misunderstanding or misapplying key scriptures makes it difficult, if not impossible, to understand what the future holds. In this chapter, we will briefly examine some such misunderstandings, especially those held by people who believe in Replacement Theology. Many books have been written on Replacement Theology, so I will just hit the highlights. Following is a brief description of the four most common viewpoints on the end times and specifically the book of Revelation:

- The *preterist view* holds the belief that the Great Tribulation happened in AD 70. Some adherents think we are already living in the millennium.

They believe that most, if not all, prophecy has been fulfilled, and that Israel has been replaced by the church. Replacement Theology shares this belief.

- The *idealist view* sees Revelation as mainly symbolic pictures that cannot be taken literally.

- The *historical view* is that Revelation is in symbolic form and is subjective in identifying symbols and historical fulfillment.

- The *futurist view* holds that there are prophecies yet to be fulfilled such as the Great Tribulation, the physical return of Jesus Christ to this earth, and the millennial kingdom. This is the literal approach to the Bible and the view to which I adhere.

Replacement Theology Views

Among the views shared by either some or all Replacement Theology proponents are . . .

- The church has replaced Israel in God's plans.

- The Abrahamic covenants have already been fulfilled or . . .

- The church is fulfilling the covenants.

- The church and Israel are the same.

- The Great Tribulation took place in AD 70.

- There are no further prophecies to be fulfilled or . . .

- We are now in the millennial period.

Are God and the Gospel Impartial?

Many seminaries teach that God and the gospel are impartial. But complete impartiality would bring this question: Has anyone ever made a promise, divine or otherwise, of a heavenly or earthly inheritance? Wouldn't any promise show partiality? Impartiality may sound good in theory, but in reality, it is misleading.

The only time impartiality makes sense is in the context of salvation: God's grace is the same for everyone.

God has made promises to Israel, and because He cannot lie, He will keep those covenants. Consider this: If God broke the covenant with His chosen people because of their disobedience, how could we be sure He would keep His promise for our salvation? God always has and always will keep His promises!

The People of Israel: Still God's Chosen People

Seminaries and those who teach that the church and Israel are one fail to understand the promise God made to Abraham: Someday the land would belong to Israel. There are no promises to the Body of Christ regarding ownership of land.

Some try to make their point with Scripture passages taken out of context. Let me give two references showing how easily Scripture can be twisted.

> For the promise that he would be the heir of the world *was* not to Abraham or to his seed through

> the law, but through the righteousness of faith.
> (Romans 4:13)

In light of this verse, some think the church, not Israel, will inherit the promises. They try to support their claim that the church receives the promise by misusing the phrase "the righteousness of faith."

This verse says nothing that would exclude Abraham, Isaac, Jacob, and all Abraham's physical seed, the Jewish people. It is talking about the law, which was severe, a bondage to Israel. Let's look at the next verse.

> For if those who are of the law *are* heirs, faith is made void and the promise made of no effect. (Romans 4:14)

Paul said this when writing to the church of Galatia: "So then, brethren, we are not children of the bondwoman but of the free" (Galatians 4:31).

Both Jews and Gentiles are free from the law through faith; a second reference is found in Romans.

> And if some of the branches were broken off, and you, being a wild olive tree, were grafted in among them, and with them became a partaker of the root and fatness of the olive tree, do not boast against the branches. But if you do boast, *remember that* you do not support the root, but the root *supports* you. (Romans 11:17–18)

Based on this verse, some think the church is now part of the same olive tree as Israel. Since Israel as a nation rejected

Jesus, believers in Replacement Theology claim the church is now fulfilling the role originally given to Israel.

However, this scripture is not referring to just any olive tree but a "wild olive tree" that would, in all likelihood, bear little if any fruit. Gentiles were bearing little fruit or no fruit at all, while the Israelites were the chosen people who enjoyed the promise made to Abraham.

Israel had everything going for it, but many in the nation rejected Jesus as God. Because of their unbelief, "some of the branches were broken off." This refers to the Jews. The phrase "you, being a wild olive tree, were grafted in among them" is directed to the Gentiles. God took in the Gentiles—at that time called "dogs" by the Jews—and graciously offered them the fatness of Abraham's promise. Yet one day God is going to return to His covenant people, Israel.

> For if you were cut out of the olive tree which is wild by nature, and were grafted contrary to nature into a cultivated olive tree, how much more will these, who *are* natural *branches*, be grafted into their own olive tree? (Romans 11:24)

God took the natural, broke it off, and set it aside. Meanwhile, He has grafted in branches from the old "wild olive tree," and the Gentiles have been enjoying His blessing for almost 2,000 years.

"How much more will these, who *are* natural *branches* . . .?" This phrase describes the nation of Israel and confirms that God will graft its people back "into their own olive tree." He will set Israel back into the root of Abraham, and Israel will be restored to the kingdom and enjoy the blessing.

The underground root of the olive tree represents the Old Testament, and everything aboveground, the New Testament. The Jewish people started on the lower branches, and then—because they refused to believe in Jesus and rejected Him—the Gentiles were grafted in. Later the Jews will be grafted in and become the natural branches.

Some believe the Old Testament is for Israel, and the New Testament is for Gentiles. This is another reason some think the church is replacing Israel. Yet, if you recall our earlier discussion, the New Testament clearly teaches the church is distinct from Israel.

We need to be aware of false statements some people make and be knowledgeable in the Word so we can correct this false teaching. Studying the Scriptures will help us understand God's plan so we can prepare for what will happen in the future.

✝

At first I was surprised at the number of people I spoke to who accept Replacement Theology as the truth. But then I realized God's Word warns us this would happen.

> And many will follow their destructive ways, because of whom the way of truth will be blasphemed. By covetousness they will exploit you with deceptive words; for a long time their judgment has not been idle, and their destruction does not slumber. (2 Peter 2:2–3)

How can we identify false teaching if we don't know the truth? When the Department of the Treasury hires new agents, they require the agents to study paper money so they can easily recognize the counterfeit. We are surrounded by false doctrine, and often believers cannot discern the false from the true. God expects us to study His Word so we will know the truth and recognize the counterfeit. He calls us to pray for wisdom and knowledge and grow in our walk with Him. As we prayerfully study the Word, He will reveal the truth more clearly. This will give us a deeper understanding that will equip us to recognize the difference between truth and counterfeit and to walk in power and share our faith.

Did the Great Tribulation Take Place in AD 70?

A few months after I started writing this book, I was excited about meeting with a man who was a retired preacher and seminary professor to discuss some of my topics. I was shocked to learn he believed the Great Tribulation, instead of an event yet to come, happened in AD 70. He offered as evidence a passage in Luke 21 describing Jesus' prophecy of the destruction of the temple in Jerusalem.

> But when you see Jerusalem surrounded by armies, then know that its desolation is near. Then let those who are in Judea flee to the mountains, let those who are in the midst of her depart, and let not those who are in the country enter her. (Luke 21:20–21)

Everything Jesus prophesied in these verses did happen in AD 70, including every stone being removed (Matthew 24:2). Below is a brief history of the destruction that occurred in AD

70 and reasons those who embrace Replacement Theology believe most if not all prophecy has been fulfilled.

The Historic Account of the Temple Being Destroyed in AD 70

Roman soldiers under Vespasian and his son General Titus, charged with putting down the Jewish rebellion, had surrounded Jerusalem and were about to start killing the Jews. Then Emperor Nero died in Rome, initiating a power struggle that led to a succession of three emperors during AD 69. At the end of the power struggle, Vespasian was declared emperor and Titus returned to finish suppressing Jewish resistance by laying siege to Jerusalem. The Christians were told to flee. An estimated 100,000 Christian Jews took the opportunity to leave the city even though the Roman soldiers were there. More than 600,000 Jews were killed.

Those who believe the Great Tribulation happened in AD 70 often quote Luke 21. Part of Jesus' prophecy in Luke 21:5–24 was fulfilled then. This was *a* tribulation. However, in verse 25 Jesus shifted from the events of AD 70 to the events that will occur during the coming seven-year Great Tribulation period (Luke 21:25–38).

Prophecies Yet to Be Fulfilled

After Jesus left the temple, the disciples went to Him privately, requesting what we would call a *one-on-one*. They asked Him, "And what *will be* the sign of Your coming, and of the end of the age?" (Matthew 24:3).

In Matthew 24:3–31, Jesus answered their questions. He talked about the end of the age, using the word *tribulation,* declaring that stars will fall from heaven and we will see the Son of Man return. These things did not happen in AD 70. They are yet to come.

Then in Matthew 24:4–51 Jesus describes the Great Tribulation. Similar descriptions of the Great Tribulation are in Revelation as well as Old Testament prophecies.

Believers of Replacement Theology and the preterist viewpoint will not agree with what I say here. I have even heard educated Bible teachers claim the book of Revelation was written by uneducated men who may not have known the difference between a thousand years and a million years. They believe we should not study the book of Revelation. But since I believe all Scripture is the inspired Word of God, I will continue to quote scriptures from different books in the Bible—including Revelation—that confirm that the Great Tribulation is in the future. Prophecies about events leading up to the Great Tribulation are now being fulfilled at a rapid pace.

Compare these scriptures found in Matthew and Revelation.

> And Jesus answered and said to them: "Take heed that no one deceives you. For many will come in My name, saying, 'I am the Christ,' and will deceive many." (Matthew 24:4–5)

> And I looked, and behold, a white horse. He who sat on it had a bow; and a crown was given to

him, and he went out conquering and to conquer.
(Revelation 6:2)

This verse in Revelation describes one of the deceivers Jesus was talking about in Matthew. The impostor even rides a white horse, which Christ will do in the end. The term *white horse* is symbolic, indicating power. The Antichrist will have supernatural power for a short time. This person, called by many names, will be a deceiver who seeks to imitate Christ. Second John 1:7 calls him "a deceiver and an antichrist."

Then Jesus made a statement in Matthew 24:6 about "wars and rumors of wars." A similar statement in Revelation 6:4 describes the deeds of the rider of the red horse and people being killed.

We read in Matthew 24:7 about "famines, pestilence, and earthquakes in various places." And Revelation 6:6 refers to a food shortage: "a quart of wheat for a denarius." Some scholars interpret this as a day's wages for a loaf of bread.

> And He will send His angels with a great sound of a trumpet, and they will gather together His elect from the four winds, from one end of heaven to the other. (Matthew 24:31)

> After these things, I saw four angels standing at the four corners of the earth, holding the four winds of the earth, that the wind should not blow on the earth, on the sea, or on any tree. (Revelation 7:1)

Jesus calls the tribulation by name in Matthew 24:9,

21, and 29. He also says, "And this gospel of the kingdom will be preached in all the world, as a witness to all the nations, and then the end will come" (Matthew 24:14). Everyone will have heard the gospel before the end of the Great Tribulation. When the gospel is preached in all the world, the Great Commission will have been completed.

Before closing this chapter, we will look at verses from the writings of Amos, who prophesied around 800 BC. This was during a time of optimism when King Uzziah sat on the throne of Judah. Business was booming, boundaries were bulging—and hypocritical religious notions had replaced true worship. Amos tried to warn the Jews that God would punish them for living in sin. He reminded them that God had delivered them out of Egypt but warned that judgment would fall on Israel if the people did not repent. (We must realize God judges every nation for sin and unbelief, as well as its failure to honor Him. Even the United States is not exempt from such judgment.)

> "I will bring back the captives of My people Israel;
> They shall build the waste cities and inhabit *them;*
> They shall plant vineyards and drink wine from
> them; They shall also make gardens and eat fruit
> from them. I will plant them in their land, And
> no longer shall they be pulled up From the land
> I have given them," Says the LORD your God.
> (Amos 9:14–15)

God was talking about His people, Israel. Their land was a wasteland for over 1800 years, from the fall of Jerusalem in AD 70 until about 180 years ago when fourteen Jewish people were the first to return and settle there. At that time, the land was arid, unable to support vegetation. However, we have seen a great change in the land of Israel over the last several years. People are planting vineyards and gardens. Orchards are being blessed with such an overflowing harvest that they can now export many crops. God is also bringing them back home from places around the globe in record numbers. He will not remove them from their land.

Many nations are against Israel—just look at how the United Nations votes. Other nations lust after this tiny plot of land. Just before the end, when their enemies think they are about to destroy Israel, God will supernaturally defend them. The results will be tragic for their enemies.

The Nation of Israel and the Body of Christ

We can only interpret the Scriptures accurately when we keep the nation of Israel and the Body of Christ separate in our minds.

Abraham's physical seed are a special, called-out, separate, covenant people of God, and God has made unique promises to them. The Body of Christ (church-age believers) are also special, but different.

Jesus came to save both Jews and Gentiles—but He has a different role for each to play in this world. Gentiles and Jews who receive Christ and follow Him—the Body of Christ—are referred to as heirs of God through Christ (Galatians 4:7).

God promised Israel their land, and we must be on guard when anyone makes comments that equate Israel with the church. No, the church is not Israel, and Israel is not the church. There must be no confusion about that.

In Luke 21:24, Jesus spoke of the Gentiles taking control "until the times of the Gentiles are fulfilled." Even after Israel was recognized as a nation on May 14, 1948, Gentiles continue to influence some of that nation's decisions. But in the last days, the times of the Gentiles will end and the people of Israel will once again lead God's army of believers.

chapter 3

The Mosaic Covenant and the New Covenant

Most of God's covenants with His chosen people were unconditional. The Mosaic covenant is the one exception: This covenant was conditional on Israel's obedience (Exodus 19:5–6). It required them to obey God. If they did, they would be "a special treasure" to God; if not, they would face judgment and loss.

God gave the Mosaic covenant to help us understand sin. The Ten Commandments were perfect—they were from God. However, man's sinful heart is not capable of perfection, and everyone falls short of keeping the commandments.

The law had no power to save anyone in the Old Testament any more than it does now. Rather, it served as a vivid reminder of humankind's need for a Savior (Hebrews 11:9–10). It was faith that God counted for righteousness—faith not only to believe *in* God but also to believe God. "Just as Abraham '*believed God, and it was accounted to him for righteousness*'" (Galatians 3:6).

The Mosaic covenant was between God and Israel (Exodus 19). The problem at Mount Sinai was not in God's provision of the law but in Israel's response.

New Covenant Promised to Israel

Long after the Abrahamic and Mosaic covenants, the prophet Isaiah mentioned another covenant to be made with Israel in the future—an everlasting covenant. The term *Israel* refers to the descendants of Abraham.

> "For I, the LORD, love justice; I hate robbery for burnt offering; I will direct their work in truth, And will make with them an everlasting covenant." (Isaiah 61:8)

Some years later, Jeremiah told more about this new covenant yet to come.

> "Behold, the days are coming, says the LORD, when I will make a new covenant with the house of Israel and with the house of Judah— not according to the covenant that I made with their fathers in the day *that* I took them by the hand to lead them out of the land of Egypt, My covenant which they broke, though I was a husband to them, says the LORD. But this *is* the covenant that I will make with the house of Israel after those days, says the LORD: I will put My law in their minds, and write it on their hearts; and I will be their God, and they shall be My people." (Jeremiah 31:31–33)

Jeremiah 31 shows us the old covenant had been recognized as inadequate and states that God would someday make a new covenant with Israel. With Israel, not with the church.

And then in Ezekiel 37:21–28 is yet another prophecy

about the new covenant God would make with "the children of Israel" (v. 21). Here is a portion of that prophecy.

> "Moreover I will make a covenant of peace with them, and it shall be an everlasting covenant with them; I will establish them and multiply them, and I will set My sanctuary in their midst forevermore." (Ezekiel 37:26)

At the Last Supper, Jesus explained the new covenant was His blood shed for the remission of our sins.

> Likewise He also *took* the cup after supper, saying, "This cup *is* the new covenant in My blood, which is shed for you." (Luke 22:20)

Hebrews 8 quotes from the Jeremiah 31 prophecy. The author of Hebrews refers to the new covenant and describes the Mosaic covenant as "growing old and ready to vanish away."

> In that He says, "A *new covenant*," He has made the first obsolete. Now what is becoming obsolete and growing old is ready to vanish away. (Hebrew 8:13)

Some say the new covenant was for the church, but Scripture clearly states the new covenant was made with the nation of Israel.

First to the Jews—and Then to the Gentiles

> For I am not ashamed of the gospel of Christ, for it is the power of God to salvation for everyone

> who believes, for the Jew first and also for the
> Greek. (Romans 1:16)

The new covenant, a promise of God's grace and salvation by faith, was made first to the Jew—and then to the Greek (representing Gentiles). God didn't take His promise away from Israel to give to the Gentiles. As we've seen in the scriptures discussed, the new covenant with Israel was an everlasting one. It was simply expanded to include the Gentiles.

The twelve apostles understood the new covenant would be for them (Jews), and they were ready to accept it. To begin with, they preached only to Jews—and they continued in Jewish tradition. Peter and John had been with Jesus after His resurrection and were witnesses of His ascension to heaven (Acts 1:10). But they continued going to the temple for worship: "Now Peter and John went up together to the temple at the hour of prayer, the ninth *hour*" (Acts 3:1).

These apostles were following the Jewish tradition of going to the temple to pray at a set time. At that time (this was after they had seen Jesus ascend to heaven) Peter had not yet grasped the concept of the New Testament church or the impartiality of salvation for both Jews and Gentiles. It was only later that Paul revealed the mystery that had so long been misunderstood—that both Jews and Gentiles were to have equal status in the church, the Body of Christ (Ephesians 3:1–6; Colossians 1:25–27).

From Scripture, we can see Peter was still trying to live by the law eighteen-plus years after Christ's resurrection. (We will support this claim with scriptures in chapter six.)

Then God vividly showed Peter that Gentiles could also be saved. He sent the reluctant apostle to share the gospel with Cornelius's household.

Soon after that, Peter had to defend himself to the apostles and brethren in Judea who felt he had made a mistake by going to the Gentiles (Acts 11:1–3). A footnote in my NKJV says, "The Jews were not fond of the Gentiles. In some rabbinical writing, the Gentiles were considered to have been created by God to kindle the fires of hell. They were called dogs (Matthew 15:26) and unclean (10:14)." However, Peter's God-ordained experience with Cornelius and his household had changed his perspective. He saw salvation come to this Gentile household. Read his words and the response of his accusers:

> "If therefore God gave them the same gift as *He gave* us when we believed on the Lord Jesus Christ, who was I that I could withstand God?" When they heard these things they became silent; and they glorified God, saying, "Then God has also granted to the Gentiles repentance to life." (Acts 11:17–18)

Salvation for All

Although the new covenant was made with the Jews, salvation through faith in Christ is a spiritual promise and a blessing for all who turn to Jesus. The forgiveness of sin and salvation accompanied by the presence of the Holy Spirit are for both Jews and Gentiles.

The shed blood of Jesus made a way for believers to access the blessing and to take part in the Lord's Supper. In 1 Corinthians 11:24–25, Jesus told His disciples to "do this in remembrance of Me."

Because Jesus shed His blood, the Body of Christ benefits from the new covenant as joint-heirs with Christ in the household of faith and has access to all the rights and privileges of salvation. As Christians, we enjoy this in spirit, not in the letter of the law. Therefore, unlike Israel, who will go through the Great Tribulation, we receive the blessing of the new covenant without enduring that terrible hardship. The covenant with Israel will be completed in the millennium.

Passover Seder

We will close this chapter by comparing the relationship between the new covenant and the Jewish Passover Seder (also known as *Pesach*).This is the meal Jesus was observing at the Last Supper with His disciples before His crucifixion. (If you are not familiar with the Seder meal, you should find this interesting.)

In Exodus 6:6–8, God told Israel He would free them from captivity in Egypt but would require something of them first. At God's instruction (Exodus 12) Moses told the people to apply the blood of a lamb to the lintels and doorposts of their homes so the angel of death would *pass over* them (see Exodus 12:13). This shows us how God graciously makes a way of escape for those who are His.

Listed below are some ingredients used in the Passover

Seder the Jewish people celebrate to commemorate the exodus from Egypt. Christians take part in communion to celebrate salvation through Yeshua (Hebrew for Jesus). Both Jews and Christians celebrate God's deliverance from bondage—the Jews' deliverance from bondage to Egypt and every believer's deliverance from bondage to sin.

The foods eaten at a Seder meal are symbolic.

- Maror (bitter herbs) symbolizes the bitterness of slavery.
- Karpas (parsley) dipped in salty water recalls the tears of servitude.
- Roasted egg symbolizes life.
- The lamb shank bone represents the sacrificial lamb.
- Haroset (an apple nut mix) symbolizes the mortar the Hebrews used to make bricks for the Egyptians.

Before the Seder meal, the Jews clean their houses searching for any remnants of leaven, which represents sin. During the meal, three pieces of unleavened bread are set on the table. The center piece of the three is the *afikomen*, which is set aside. The unleavened bread, called *matzo*, is striped and pierced when baked, reminding Christians of the stripes Yeshua received from the whips of the Roman guards and the piercing of a sword. Isaiah prophesied this in Isaiah 53:5–8, and we read of the fulfillment in John 19:39. At one point in the meal, the matzo is taken out and broken in half, wrapped in linen, and hidden, just as Yeshua's body was wrapped in linen and hidden in the grave. Later, with much joy and excitement, the children search and find the *afikomen,* and the father rewards the one who discovers it. After the temple was destroyed in AD 70 and no more sacrifices could be made, the *afikomen* became the substitute for the Passover lamb.

As believers, we are thankful that Yeshua became the last, perfect Passover lamb. He was the only sinless Man who ever lived, which also made Him the only One who could redeem mankind. Man can never be God, but God can become Man. His sacrifice paid the penalty for the sins of the whole world. It is heartbreaking to know that most people will reject Him.

The Last Supper, also called the *Pesach* meal, is a beautiful reminder of the sacrificial gift of Yeshua's life. It is believed that Yeshua, the Lamb of God, was crucified at the very time the Passover lambs were being offered on the Temple Mount. The supper is also a memorial, forever commemorating the redemption of the firstborn children of Israel on the night before the exodus. Jesus served the Last Supper on the anniversary of the Hebrews' deliverance from bondage to Egypt.

There is much more to the *Pesach* meal, but we will end by mentioning the five cups of wine served at the dinner. One is the cup recorded in Matthew 26:27–29 during the Lord's Supper. This is the cup the Body of Christ takes during the sacrament of Communion.

- The first cup—the Cup of Sanctification, *Kiddush* in Hebrew, signifies the Jews being brought out of bondage. A blessing is recited before the meal that acknowledges and honors God as the source of all good. This prayer consecrates the occasion and the meal to God. It is associated with the first promise God gave to the people of Israel: "I will bring you out from under the burdens of the Egyptians" (Exodus 6:6).

- The second cup is based on the promise that "I will rescue you from their bondage" (Exodus 6:6). It comes after the story of the exodus when the ten plagues are recited. This cup of wine represents joy. Each time a plague is mentioned, the level of wine in the cup goes down when everyone dips a finger into his or her cup and dries it on a napkin. It also represents an expression of sympathy for the Egyptians. This cup is called the Cup of Praise and Deliverance.

- The third cup is the Cup of Redemption, which symbolizes the blood of the Passover lamb with which the Messiah (Jesus) identified Himself. It is based on the third promise: "I will redeem you with an outstretched arm and great judgments" (Exodus 6:6). Jesus fulfilled this when, as the Lamb of God, He stretched out His arms on the cross. This third cup is the one we celebrate when we partake of Communion at church.

  In the same manner *He* also *took* the cup after supper, saying, "This cup is the new covenant in My blood. This do, as often as you drink *it*, in remembrance of Me." (1 Corinthians 11:25)

- The fourth cup is called the Cup of Completion and represents the promise, "I will take you as My people and I will be your God" (Exodus 6:7). It is followed by reciting some or all of the *Hallel*. Psalms 113–118 constitute the Hallel (praise) of the Jewish festivals. Bible scholars believe Jesus and His disciples may have sung a hymn from the Hallel at the conclusion of their Passover meal before going out to the garden on the Mount of Olives (Matthew 26:30; Mark 14:26).

• The fifth cup is the Cup for Elijah, which is filled and waiting for him. At the end of the Seder meal, children open the front door and call for Elijah. His cup is not consumed but is included in the Seder to represent their expectation that Elijah will return with the Messiah at Passover. An empty chair is set for him.

> Behold, I will send you Elijah the prophet Before the coming of the great and dreadful day of the LORD. (Malachi 4:5)

Most Jewish people are still waiting for their Messiah. Unfortunately, they deny that He has already come. The truth is that Jesus, the Messiah, will return and will drink that cup with believers.

We often hear Matthew 26:26–28 read when we observe the Lord's Supper. These verses should bring tears to our eyes as we realize Jesus Christ is waiting to drink that cup with us, His followers.

> "But I say to you, I will not drink of this fruit of the vine from now on until that day when I drink it new with you in My Father's kingdom." (Matthew 26:29)

chapter 4

Old Testament History

In the Old Testament, we read prophecies of wars, curses, and blessings—including the birth of Jesus. Zechariah prophesied Christ would triumphantly enter Jerusalem as king (Zechariah 9:9). Fulfillment of this prophecy is recorded in Matthew 21:1–5, Mark 11:1–10, and John 12:12–19. Most Jews were waiting and watching for this event—and yet many missed it.

The death of Jesus was also prophesied. The rabbis did not grasp the real meaning of the prophecies. They had a problem with someone who would suffer death at the hands of his enemy yet rule as their king. Some of the Jewish leaders mistakenly thought there might be two deliverers: one to suffer (Isaiah 53) and one to rule (Isaiah 63). They wanted a king to take charge of the government and free them from the abuses they had been suffering from the Roman government.

Many of the Old Testament prophecies have been fulfilled. Some have not but will be. Studying Old Testament history and prophecies can help us learn from the past, live more effectively in the present, and prepare for the future.

A Quick View of Old Testament History: The Beginnings

Genesis 1–11 covers the first two thousand years of history. It describes the creation and the first sin by Adam (Genesis 3:6). In Genesis 3:15, God presents the plan of salvation for us. Genesis 4:8 recounts the first murder. Then comes a description of the flood that destroyed a thoroughly sinful world. God saved the only eight righteous people to restart mankind.

Two hundred and fifty years later, God scattered mankind at the Tower of Babel because of their sin and idol worship. Their excessive pride had spurred them into trying to "make a name" for themselves (Genesis 11:1–9). Various cultures developed and nations grew. And—typical of the human race—sin and idolatry prevailed.

This is also believed to be the time astrology began. Astrologers considered themselves so smart they thought they could predict the future. Even Abraham's father had other gods.

> And Joshua said to all the people, "Thus says the LORD God of Israel: 'Your fathers, *including* Terah, the father of Abraham and the father of Nahor, dwelt on the other side of the River in old times; and they served other gods.'" (Joshua 24:2)

A New Race: God's Chosen People

God called Abraham to serve Him and become the father of the Jewish race.

When Abraham (then called Abram) was first called,

he moved from Ur of the Chaldeans in southern Babylonia (Genesis 11:31) north along the trade route and crossed over the Euphrates river, eventually settling in Haran. God chose this seventy-five-year-old patriarch to follow Him and begin a new people. God promised his descendants would become a great nation (Genesis 12:1–3).

Abraham believed God and moved to the land of Canaan. He believed God's promise that this land would belong to his descendants even though the Canaanites were in the land (Psalm 105:8–9). This was the start of Abraham's faith-filled journey. He was an important figure in the history of God's people Israel. The covenant God made with him thousands of years ago continues to affect our world today.

Abraham was the father of Isaac and Jacob and all their descendants. Jacob was later called Israel, and his twelve sons became the twelve tribes of Israel about 2000 BC.

In Egypt: From Seventy to a Multitude

God used a famine and His faithful servant Joseph (Jacob's son) to bring Jacob and his other sons to Egypt. Their descendants remained in Egypt for about 400 years, growing from a household of 70 to a multitude of more than 600,000 men over age twenty plus women and children. Eventually God called Moses to free them from Egyptian slavery.

The Israelites wandered in the wilderness for the next 40 years—because even with the miracles God did to free them and to keep them, they were unfaithful to Him. During this time, around 1500 BC, God gave Moses the Ten

Commandments, which served as a measuring stick to reveal that every living person falls short of His commands.

Finally, Joshua led God's chosen people into the Promised Land. Through the years, they continued to go through cycles of faithfulness followed by rebellion. Again and again. God raised up judges to guide them. And then they insisted on having kings like other countries.

David appeared on the scene in Israel about 1000 BC. He became king after King Saul. David's son Solomon built the first temple over a forty-year time span. A beautiful temple, it was used for about four hundred years. During that time, the people of Israel continued a path of sin and rebellion. They did not even keep the Sabbath.

> And the LORD spoke to Moses, saying, "Speak also to the children of Israel, saying: 'Surely My Sabbaths you shall keep, for it *is* a sign between Me and you throughout your generations, that *you* may know that I *am* the LORD who sanctifies you.'" (Exodus 31:12–13)

God told them to work and harvest the land for six years. On the seventh year, the Sabbath year, they were to leave the land idle. But they did not observe the Sabbath year. They lived there for 490 years. During that time, they failed to observe 70 Sabbath years (490 divided by seven). This led to seventy years of captivity by the Babylonian Empire. God blesses people and tells them to follow what He says; the consequence is theirs if they do not obey.

God Warned the People through Jeremiah

God sent His prophet Jeremiah to His people to warn them to repent. He reminded them they had forgotten God and had failed to listen for His voice. He also accused both religious and civic leaders of abandoning God's agenda. Jeremiah decried the apostasy of God's chosen people and predicted their future.

> And this whole land shall be a desolation *and* an astonishment, and these nations shall serve the king of Babylon seventy years. (Jeremiah 25:11)

If Jeremiah were here today, he could be preaching the same sermon to us. Would we listen and believe—or turn our backs as the people did in his day?

Exile

God had blessed Israel greatly in the previous years, but because He was angry with them as a nation, He raised up Nebuchadnezzar from Babylon to destroy Jerusalem. People in the Babylonian Empire were the worst of sinners. They destroyed almost everything in Jerusalem in 606 BC, taking the best of the young men—including Daniel—and women into captivity. The third time they came back, between 589–586 BC, they destroyed Jerusalem and the temple. This was the start of Gentiles ruling over the Jews—and they remained under Gentile rule in various nations and under a variety of rulers for centuries. God used the evil nation Babylon to kill and scatter His people, but He did not let the nation that punished His people go unpunished themselves (Jeremiah 25:12).

Babylon was so powerful its leaders thought they could rule forever. The palace was surrounded by a brick wall (I have read that you could drive chariots on top of it). The water they used was routed around and under the buildings and inside the compound.

King Nebuchadnezzar (Daniel 2 and 3) made an image of gold and told everyone that at the sound of horns, flutes, and other music, they must fall down and worship the image. When the music was played, three Israelites named Shadrach, Meshach, and Abed-Nego did not obey. These men were Jews who had been placed over the affairs of the province of Babylon.

The Chaldeans accused them before the king, stating the three Hebrews did not bow down to worship their gods or the gold image Nebuchadnezzar had set up. They were then brought before the king, who gave them another chance.

When they again refused to bow, he raged with anger. He ordered them thrown into one of those furnaces built into the massive brick wall surrounding the palace and commanded his soldiers to turn up the furnace seven times hotter. The king's men bound Shadrach, Meshach, and Abed-Nego in their clothes, coats, and even their turbans, and then threw them into the fire. The fire was so hot it killed the king's men (Daniel 3:22).

Later, King Nebuchadnezzar asked if they had thrown only three men into the furnace because he observed a fourth figure in the searing flames.

> I see four men loose, walking in the midst of the
> fire; and they are not hurt, and the form of the
> fourth is like the Son of God. (Daniel 3:25)

The men were brought out of the furnace. Miracle of miracles! Not only were they not burned, their hair was not singed nor was there even the smell of smoke on them.

Who was the fourth person the king had seen? Jesus made several preincarnate visits to earth, known as Christophanies. It may be that the fourth person was our Savior—protecting Shadrach, Meshach, and Abed-Nego from the raging fire.

Moved by what had happened, the king issued a national decree to worship the true God, and the three Hebrew men were promoted to a higher position in Babylon. (Read the entire story in Daniel 3:1–30.)

In later years, under the rule of Darius, God again intervened to save His faithful servant Daniel from certain death when he was thrown into the lions' den.

King Belshazzar and Cyrus

Some years later, Belshazzar (Nebuchadnezzar's grandson) gave a feast for thousands of his lords. The gold vessels that had been taken from the temple in Jerusalem were brought out of storage and used that night. This angered God. The king was astonished to see the fingers of a man's hand writing on the wall. He called Daniel to interpret this writing, which said that God was going to take Belshazzar's life and kingdom because of his sin. (See Daniel 5.)

Daniel March gives this account in his 1868 book, *Night Scenes in the Bible:*

> There is no more effectual way to destroy a great and mighty nation than to give its young men all the money they want, provide them with plays and festivities and amusements and dances and wine, and then leave them to sweat the life and manhood out of body and soul in the hot-bed of pleasure and self-indulgence. That is the way Babylon was ruined. That is the way imperial Rome became an easy prey to northern Barbarians. That is the way Christian Constantinople came under the debasing and abominable sway of Mohammedans. That is the way Venice ended a thousand years of independent and glorious history with shame and servitude. And nothing worse could come upon the fairest and most Christian city in the world than to have a generation of tender and delicate young men, without energy, without principle, without conscience, but with money enough to support elegant pleasure and costly vices. Let such young men give tone to public opinion, and take the lead in the highest circles of society in any city of our land, and they would soon make it the Sodom of America.[2]

> "The music and the banquet and wine; the garlands, the rose-odours, and the flowers; the sparkling eyes, the flashing ornaments, the jeweled arms, the raven hair, the braids, the bracelets, the thin robes floating like clouds; the fair forms, the delusion and the false enchantment of the dizzy scene," take away all reason and all reverence from the flushed and crowed revelers.

There is now nothing too sacred for them to profane, and Belshazzar himself takes the lead in the riot and the blasphemy. Even the mighty and terrible Nebuchadnezzar, who desolated the sanctuary of Jehovah at Jerusalem, would not use his sacred trophies in the worship of his false gods. But this weak and wicked successor of the great conqueror, excited with wine and carried away with the delusion that no foe can ever capture his great city, is anxious to make some grand display of defiant and blasphemous desecration.[3]

What else was going on that night? While Belshazzar carried on the blasphemous desecration, confident of his invincibility, the army of the Medes and Persians, led by King Cyrus, was damming up and rerouting the water around the building. They went up the muddied river channel into the city and killed Belshazzar and many of his officials. Daniel lived to serve another king.

This event fulfilled prophecy. Two hundred years before Cyrus was born, Isaiah called him by name, prophesying that Cyrus was God's shepherd. He even wrote that the gates would not be shut and that God would subdue nations before His anointed, Cyrus.

> "Who says to the deep, 'Be dry! And I will dry up your rivers'; Who says of Cyrus, '*He is* My shepherd, And he shall perform all My pleasure, Saying to Jerusalem, "You shall be built," And to the temple, "Your foundation shall be laid."' Thus says the LORD to His anointed, To Cyrus, whose right hand I have held—To subdue nations before him And loose the armor of kings, To open before

him the double doors, So that the gates will not be shut." (Isaiah 44:27–45:1)

Ken Johnson, best known for his book *Ancient Prophecies Revealed: 500 Prophecies Listed in Order of When They Were Fulfilled,* wrote this:

> Cyrus besieged Babylon but could not conquer the city. The city of Babylon had outer walls that were more than 70 feet thick, 300 feet high, with more than 250 watchtowers. It had motes [sic] and many other defenses. Since the city sat on the Euphrates River, the inhabitants had all the water and food they needed. They could withstand a siege indefinitely. If Cyrus could not scale the walls or wait them out, how could he conquer the city? Josephus writes that a group of Jews showed the prophecies to Cyrus. He learned of his destiny and was even told by Isaiah's prophecy how to breach the walls of Babylon![4]

As the new ruler, Cyrus gave his permission and financial support to the Jewish people so they could return to Jerusalem and rebuild their city and temple. It is interesting that by studying the prophecies of Jeremiah, Daniel knew about the end of the seventy years before the end of the seventieth year had taken place:

> In the first year of his reign I, Daniel, understood by the books the number of the years *specified* by the word of the LORD through Jeremiah the prophet, that He would accomplish seventy years in the desolations of Jerusalem. (Daniel 9:2)

As prophesied by Jeremiah many years before, during the first year of Cyrus's reign, he freed the people of Israel to return to their homeland and rebuild their temple.

Story of Esther

The book of Esther takes place about 470 BC. After conquering Babylon in 539 BC, Cyrus freed the Jewish people to return to their Jewish homeland, but some chose to stay in Persia. Now, years later, many Jews still lived in Persia.

Before we get into the story of Esther, a look into history would be helpful. The Scriptures talk about the evil of Balaam. God used Balaam to prophesy for Balak and Amalek, who asked him to curse Israel.

> Then he looked on Amalek, and he took up his oracle and said: "Amalek *was* first among the nations, but *shall be* last until he perishes." (Numbers 24:20)

The Amalekites were coming to their end, but Saul delayed their complete demise (1Samuel 15:5–9). Samuel told Saul the LORD had sent him to anoint Saul as king. Later, God commanded Saul to destroy all the Amalekites, not sparing any. God was angry with the Amalekites and was going to punish them because they had ambushed the Israelites when they came up from Egypt.

Did Saul obey God? No, he destroyed most of the Amalekites but spared Agag, their king, and kept the best of the livestock. God was not pleased with Saul.

Now to the book of Esther where a man named Haman appears. He was an Amalekite whose ancestors should have been destroyed but were not because of Saul's disobedience.

King Ahasuerus of Persia banished his first queen because she did not respond to his command to come to him during a drunken celebration. A widespread search for a new queen began. After viewing all the beautiful young virgin women selected from throughout the land as candidates, the king picked Esther to be his queen, not knowing she was a Jew. Mordecai, Esther's cousin, had raised her like his own daughter for she had lost her mother and father. He was watching out for her as a father would his own daughter, and he told her not to disclose that she was Jewish.

While Mordecai was sitting within the king's gate, he heard two eunuchs planning to kill the king. He told Esther (who was by then the queen), and she told the king. After confirming the charge, the two eunuchs were hanged, and "it was written in the book of chronicles in the presence of the king" (Esther 2:23).

Haman was above all the princes and second in command. Pride and ambition were his masters. When he walked by the king's servants, they would bow and pay homage to him, stroking his inflated ego. However, Mordecai would not bow or pay undue respect to Haman.

Haman was enraged by Mordecai's refusal to bow before him. Seeking revenge, he came up with a plan to have all the Jews killed. He went to the king and lied, telling him there was a group of people who should all be destroyed because they didn't keep the king's law. The king signed a decree to do so. A letter was then sent throughout the land that on a certain date, all the Jews must be killed and their land and property given to whoever killed them. This was to take place March 7, nearly a year later.

Mordecai told Esther that she had to tell the king she was Jewish and plead for him to change the order to kill all the Jews. She knew if she appeared before the king without his invitation, he could put her to death. She asked Mordecai and others to fast and pray. They did, and then she went before the king, who wanted to know her request. She replied that she wanted to have a banquet for him and Haman.

At the banquet, the king again asked Esther what she wanted. He said he would give her anything—even half the kingdom! But she just asked for him and Haman to return the next night for another banquet.

Wow! Haman was feeling good now—just the three of them for another special banquet! But on the way home, he passed Mordecai sitting at the palace gate. Still Mordecai refused to stand up or bow to honor Haman.

Haman told his wife and friends how unhappy he was. They suggested that he build a gallows, fifty cubits high, and ask the king to hang Mordecai. He could hardly wait to see the king about granting his request to do just that, and he set out for the palace.

That night, the king could not sleep. When a king cannot sleep, nobody sleeps. He ordered an attendant to read the book of history to him. When he heard from that book that Mordecai had once saved his life, he wanted to know if any honor had been bestowed on him. His attendant told him nothing had been done. Just then, the king heard a noise in the court as Haman hurried to ask the king to hang Mordecai. God's timing is always perfect.

The king told his servant to bring Haman in. The king asked Haman for ideas for honoring someone. Haman was so happy; he was sure the king wanted to honor him. After all, he was going to be at the banquet with the king and Esther. So he described an honor he craved for himself.

> "Let a royal robe be brought which the king has worn, and a horse on which the king has ridden, which has a royal crest placed on its head." (Esther 6:8)

He also told the king the man should be paraded through the city square on the horse. The king thought that was a great idea! He told Haman to follow through with these suggestions for *Mordecai the Jew.*

What a shock for Haman! The next day, he was furious as he led the very man he sought to destroy in front of the crowds on the king's horse. He was so enraged he went home with his head covered. While he was complaining to his friends and his wife, the eunuchs came to hurry him to the banquet Esther had prepared.

While enjoying the banquet, the king again wanted to know Esther's request. She told him an order had been issued to kill her and all of her people. This news upset the king. He wanted to know who would do such a thing. Esther replied that the adversary was the wicked Haman. Haman was terrified.

The king was so angry and distraught he went out to the garden to think. He came back into the room just as a despairing Haman had fallen across the couch where Esther was. "The king asked, 'Will he also assault the queen while I *am* in the house?'" (Esther 7:8).

Then one of the eunuchs told the king about the fifty-cubit high gallows Haman had made for Mordecai. The king replied, "Hang him on it." So Haman and his ten sons were hanged on the gallows he had built for Mordecai.

The book of Esther does not have the word *God* in it, but He is there. Esther, through God's divine plan and purpose, saved the Jewish race, and Mordecai was appointed to take over Haman's job. The Jews turned a day of sorrow into a day of joy. They killed and destroyed the enemies of the Jews. They called that day Purim (in Hebrew *Purim* means "lots" and refers to the lottery Haman used to choose the date for the massacre).

Purim is a Jewish holiday still celebrated today—a joyous and fun time. It commemorates a time when the Jewish people living in Persia were saved from extermination. Purim is celebrated around March 15, except in leap years, when it is always celebrated one month before Passover. During Purim, the book of Esther is read, honoring Esther as the heroine. Each time the name Haman, the villain, is read, people stamp their feet, boo, hiss, rattle cans, and make a loud racket –symbolically blotting out the name of Haman.

God used Esther, like Joseph and Moses, to deliver His people. (Read the book of Esther for the rest of the story.)

Because of Esther's intervention, the Amalekites in that area were finally destroyed. Saul had not followed God's instructions to destroy them many years before, but God's plan always happens. There are mysteries that we will never understand this side of heaven, but we can always be confident that God's Word will be fulfilled.

The Temple Rebuilt—and Again Destroyed

The Jews excelled in vocation, business, and most everything else they did. They set up synagogues, which gave them places to worship, to learn, and to help one another. Throughout history, they have been quite adaptable, and once they settle in a foreign country, most of them will stay. It is estimated that fewer than 50,000 Jews out of over a million went back from Babylon to their homes in Jerusalem to rebuild the city walls and the temple.

After the Jews were free to return from Babylon, they rebuilt the temple. This temple was not as elegant as the first one built by King Solomon. However, God later used Herod the Great to make the second temple a beautiful place to worship.

Herod liked to build things. He may have been called "the Great" because he was the oldest son of Antipater of Judea. He became governor of Galilee and established himself in the entire region. Before he could rebuild the temple, loads of dirt had to be brought in to build a retaining wall. This was a major job as the wall was made of stones, some as much as seventeen feet thick and weighing thousands of pounds. They were fitted by hand, and it was reported that over 10,000 stonecutters worked at one time, fitting each stone on top or beside another one. Archaeologists have found lead under the large stones, so they believe the builders used balls of lead to help move and place the stones. When they set stones on top, the weight flattened the lead as the stone settled.

The Roman general Titus destroyed this temple in August AD 70.

Daniel prophesied that Messiah would come before the city was destroyed, and we know the city and temple were destroyed by the Romans: "The people of the prince who is to come shall destroy the city and the sanctuary" (Daniel 9:26).

It is not clear just how the fire started at the temple, as the Romans were burning buildings all around the area. It was stated that Caesar had wanted to save the temple for his use. "And thus was the holy house burned down, without Caesar's approval."[5]

The last person to prophesy this was Jesus between AD 31 and AD 33.

> "They will not leave in you one stone upon another, because you did not know the time of your visitation." (Luke 19:44)

> "These things which you see—the days will come in which not *one* stone shall be left upon another that shall not be thrown down." (Luke 21:6)

Israel Reborn

The Jewish people remained scattered among the nations for many years. Then on May 14, 1948, we saw prophecy fulfilled (Isaiah 66:8) when Israel became a nation in one day.

Although the Jewish people suffered the consequences of their rebellion against God through the centuries, God never abandoned them. They are still His chosen people, and as we have discussed, He is bringing them back together—and He calls for us to support them.

The United States has been Israel's friend in the past, but in recent years has begun to withdraw some of its support. Our presidents—both past and present—have been involved in Israel's governmental affairs and want Israel to divide their land with the Palestinians.

God made it clear that those who help Israel will be blessed (Genesis 12:3) and those who are against Israel will be cursed. Many countries hate the Jews. According to Scripture, near the end all nations will be against them. "All the nations were deceived" (Isaiah 34:2; Joel 3; Zechariah 12:3; Matthew 24:9).

While we are talking about Israel and our support or lack of support, I would like to share some information from a conference I attended on Jerusalem.

One of the speakers, White House correspondent William Koenig, has written a book titled *Eye to Eye: Facing the Consequences of Dividing Israel*. In this book, he states repeatedly that whenever the United States puts pressure on Israel to give up some of its land, we suffer some catastrophe that costs us money—and oftentimes lives. For example, William Koenig writes,

President George W. Bush gave a major foreign

policy speech to the UN General Assembly on September 21, 2004, at 11:00 a.m. EDT. In his speech he said, "Israel should impose a settlement freeze, dismantle unauthorized outposts, end the daily humiliation of the Palestinian people, and avoid any actions that prejudice final negotiations."

From that point on, Hurricane Jeanne began a course change over the next forty-eight hours, going from its present east-northeast position in the Atlantic Ocean, moving away from the United States at the time of President Bush's speech, to be east-southeast shortly thereafter, to the southeast, south, and then west toward Florida, where it came ashore four days later as a category 3 hurricane. Hurricane Jeanne made landfall near Stuart, Florida, at midnight September 25, and into the morning hours of September 26, with 120 mph winds.[6]

The overall cost of the damage inflicted by this hurricane was estimated to be between twenty-two and twenty-five billion dollars. In the same book, Koenig tells about another incident involving former President Bush's involvement with the Middle East:

On September 10, 2001, President Bush was completing the most comprehensive Middle East peace plan ever drafted, a plan that called for a Palestinian state. No other American president had ever publicly approved a Palestinian state. President Bush was responding to Saudi Arabia's assertion that he favored Israel in the Middle East peace process.[7]

President Bush was going to sign the peace plan the next day, September 11, 2001, the day of the attack on the twin towers of the World Trade Center and the Pentagon, and the hijacking of a plane on its way to more destruction. Nearly three thousand lives were lost with an estimated cost of $222,485,000,000.[8] Life in America has never been the same.

Blessings or Curses. What Will We Choose?

God gave the land of Israel to Abraham for his descendants. If people would only read and understand the Bible, they would know that supporting Israel brings blessings but acting against Israel brings curses. It is a clear choice. What will we choose as a nation? And what will you choose as an individual?

> Now the LORD had said to Abram: "Get out of your country, From your family And from your father's house, To a land that I will show you. I will make you a great nation; I will bless you And make your name great; And you shall be a blessing. I will bless those who bless you, And I will curse him who curses you; And in you all the families of the earth shall be blessed." (Genesis 12:1–3)

chapter 5

God's Chosen People in Prophecy

I was watching Fox News in December 2009 when they announced the prime minister of Israel, Benjamin Netanyahu, was meeting a plane of Jews arriving from other countries. This planeload would bring the Jewish population to the highest percentage in the Jerusalem area in almost two thousand years.

God will never let the Jews lose that land because He gave it to them. In Ezekiel 35, we read how He will punish nations that are enemies of Israel. Chapter 36 talks about His anger with the nations surrounding Israel. It clearly shows that even though He scattered His people to punish them for their evil ways, He will bring them back at the end. Ezekiel 37 gives us a good idea of what God has done, is doing, and will do for His people.

> The hand of the LORD came upon me and brought me out in the Spirit of the LORD, and set me down in the midst of the valley; and it *was* full of bones. Then He caused me to pass by them all around, and behold, *there were* very many in the open valley; and indeed *they were* very dry. And He said

to me, "Son of man, can these bones live?" So I answered, "O Lord GOD, You know."

Again He said to me, "Prophesy to these bones, and say to them, 'O dry bones, hear the word of the LORD! Thus says the Lord GOD to these bones: "Surely I will cause breath to enter into you, and you shall live. I will put sinews on you and bring flesh upon you, cover you with skin and put breath in you; and you shall live. Then you shall know that I *am* the LORD." ' "

So I prophesied as I was commanded; and as I prophesied, there was a noise, and suddenly a rattling; and the bones came together, bone to bone. Indeed, as I looked, the sinews and the flesh came upon them, and the skin covered them over; but *there was* no breath in them. Also He said to me, "Prophesy to the breath, prophesy, son of man, and say to the breath, 'Thus says the Lord GOD: "Come from the four winds, O breath, and breathe on these slain, that they may live." ' " So I prophesied as He commanded me, and breath came into them, and they lived, and stood upon their feet, an exceedingly great army.

Then He said to me, "Son of man, these bones are the whole house of Israel. They indeed say, 'Our bones are dry, our hope is lost, and we ourselves are cut off!' Therefore prophesy and say to them, 'Thus says the Lord GOD: "Behold, O My people, I will open your graves and cause you to come up from your graves, and bring you into the land of Israel. Then you shall know that I *am* the LORD, when I have opened your graves, O My people, and brought you up from your graves. I will put My Spirit in you, and you shall live, and I will place you in your own land. Then you shall know that I, the LORD, have spoken *it* and performed *it*," says the LORD."' (Ezekiel 37:1–14)

It appears to me that the dry bones represent the Jewish people coming back into their own land of Israel after being dispersed throughout the world. In verses 12 and 13 God talks about bringing His people Israel back into the land.

> "Therefore prophesy and say to them, 'Thus says the Lord GOD: "Behold, O My people, I will open your graves and cause you to come up from your graves, and bring you into the land of Israel. Then you shall know that I *am* the LORD, when I have opened your graves, O My people, and brought you up from your graves. I will put My Spirit in you, and you shall live, and I will place you in your own land. Then you shall know that I, the LORD, have spoken *it* and performed *it*," says the LORD."' (Ezekiel 37:12–14)

They are scattered and have been spiritually dead for a long time. God will bring His people back to Jerusalem from all nations, and they will know the Lord is doing it. He will put His Spirit in them and bring them back to the land He gave to Abraham with His covenant.

> "Then say to them, 'Thus says the Lord GOD: "Surely I will take the children of Israel from among the nations, wherever they have gone, and will gather them from every side and bring them into their own land."'" (Ezekiel 37:21)

This prophecy is especially exciting because we see in the news today that the Jews are returning to Israel in greater numbers every year. They seem to sense an urgent need to move back. Fund-raising groups help needy families; some do legal work for them, making it possible for them to return to their homeland. Ministry to Israel is one of the organizations actively helping Jews from around the world return to their homeland. Here is an excerpt from their website:

CHRISTIAN PEOPLE HELPING JEWISH PEOPLE HOME - THE FINAL EXODUS

In the past few decades millions of Jews have made their way home to Israel. Since 1989, over one million have come from the former Soviet Union alone, and many more will immigrate in the next few years from around the world. Partnering with other Christian organizations worldwide, Ministry to Israel has been instrumental in assisting with the return of thousands of Jewish people to their homeland. From the first steps of the complicated and costly emigration process to arranging transportation to Israel, Christians are there to help. Local pastors and churches are utilized in facilitating each phase of the exodus in their particular country or region.[9]

Many of these people have never lived in Israel before, yet—despite all the killing and violence in that area—they still desire to live in their homeland. God is bringing back His people as prophesied. Prophecy is being fulfilled daily in front of us.

"Dem Bones"

"Dem Bones," a popular song in the 1940s and still sung today, was written by author and songwriter James Weldon Johnson in the 1800s to describe the vision God gave Ezekiel.

> The toe bone connected to the foot bone,
> The foot bone connected to the leg bone,
> The leg bone connected to the knee bone,
> The knee bone connected to the thigh bone,
> The thigh bone connected to the back bone,
> The back bone connected to the neck bone,
> The neck bone connected to the head bone,
> Oh, hear the word of the Lord!

> Dem bones, dem bones gonna walk aroun'
> Dem bones, dem bones, gonna walk aroun'
> Dem bones, dem bones, gonna walk aroun'
> Oh, hear the word of the Lord.

> The head bone connected to the neck bone,
> The neck bone connected to the back bone,
> The back bone connected to the thigh bone,
> The thigh bone connected to the knee bone,
> The knee bone connected to the leg bone,
> The leg bone connected to the heel bone,
> The heel bone connected to the foot bone,
> The foot bone connected to the toe bone,
> Oh, hear the word of the Lord!

Just picture it. Those dry bones began to shake, rattle, and roll—a picture of the people of Israel, who had been out of their promised land for centuries. God was bringing them back to life and back to their homeland. Paul wrote in Romans 11:15 that their "acceptance *be* but life from the dead." Israel's rejection is not final and never was meant to be.

> Again He said to me, "Prophesy to these bones, and say to them, 'O dry bones, hear the word of the LORD! Thus says the Lord GOD to these bones: "Surely I will cause breath to enter into you, and you shall live. I will put sinews on you and bring flesh upon you, cover you with skin and put breath in you; and you shall live. Then you shall know that I *am* the LORD.""" So I prophesied as I was commanded; and as I prophesied, there was a noise, and suddenly a rattling; and the bones came together, bone to bone. (Ezekiel 37:4–7)

God promised to give *breath* to these bones. This can be interpreted as *wind* or *spirit*. God would put *spirit* in them and restore them physically and spiritually. The whole nation has been spiritually dead, but God will restore them to life—and they will know He is God.

End Times

Some Bible scholars believe Ezekiel 37 was fulfilled at the Holocaust. But God said He would bring the Jewish people to the land of Israel and they would know He is God. I believe this refers to the end times. Verse 14 talks about their land and states they shall know the Lord has spoken. I think this is referring to the millennium, when they will know the Lord beyond any doubt.

"Then they shall dwell in the land that I have given to Jacob My servant, where your fathers dwelt; and they shall dwell there, they, their children, and their children's children, forever; and My servant David *shall be* their prince forever. Moreover I will make a covenant of peace with them, and it shall be an everlasting covenant with them; I will establish them and multiply them, and I will set My sanctuary in their midst forevermore. My tabernacle also shall be with them; indeed I will be their God, and they shall be My people. The nations also will know that I, the LORD, sanctify Israel, when My sanctuary is in their midst forevermore." (Ezekiel 37:25–28)

This passage mentions the "everlasting covenant" and the "tabernacle." God says, "I will set My sanctuary in their midst forevermore." I believe *forevermore* begins with the millennium and moves on into eternity. Jesus' return will signify the fulfillment of the old covenants and the beginning of the new. "I will make a covenant of peace with them, and it shall be an everlasting covenant with them."

"They shall not defile themselves anymore with their idols, nor with their detestable things, nor with any of their transgressions; but I will deliver them from all their dwelling places in which they have sinned, and will cleanse them. Then they shall be My people, and I will be their God." (Ezekiel 37:23)

Jeremiah also wrote about this new covenant.

"Behold, the days are coming, says the LORD,

> when I will make a new covenant with the
> house of Israel and with the house of Judah—not
> according to the covenant that I made with their
> fathers in the day *that* I took them by the hand to
> lead them out of the land of Egypt, My covenant
> which they broke, though I was a husband to
> them, says the LORD. But this *is* the covenant that
> I will make with the house of Israel after those
> days, says the LORD: I will put My law in their
> minds, and write it on their hearts; and I will be
> their God, and they shall be My people. No more
> shall every man teach his neighbor, and every man
> his brother, saying, 'Know the LORD,' for they all
> shall know Me, from the least of them to the
> greatest of them, says the LORD. For I will forgive
> their iniquity, and their sin I will remember no
> more." (Jeremiah 31:31–34)

God says His people will know He is the Lord. This will
happen in the future. The Jews still think this will be the
Messiah's first coming, but when they see Jesus, they will
recognize Him.

God will bring His people back from all over the world
and will cleanse them from their iniquity. All nations will
know they are His people. During the millennium, He will
live with them, and they will be His people forevermore.

> "As for Me," says the LORD, "this *is* My covenant
> with them: My Spirit who *is* upon you, and My
> words which I have put in your mouth, shall not
> depart from your mouth, nor from the mouth of
> your descendants, nor from the mouth of your
> descendants' descendants," says the LORD, "from
> this time and forevermore." (Isaiah 59:21)

chapter 6

Fulfillment of the Law

The Bible is a progressive revelation. The time from Adam to the flood encompassed about 1600 years. During that time, sin grew and eventually the entire human race except Noah and his family (eight people) rebelled against their Creator. After the flood, Noah's descendants rapidly multiplied. We read that 200 years later, the entire human race was again steeped in idolatry and false religion. Then came the Tower of Babel, the diversity of languages, and dispersion to many parts of the world. And people continued to rebel against God.

God went in another direction and appeared to one righteous man. He chose a man called Abram (God later changed his name to Abraham) to start a separate nation. He appeared to Abram with instructions and made a covenant. "Then the LORD appeared to Abram" (Genesis 12:7). According to Bible scholar Les Feldick, the root word for *appeared* is *optomai*, from which we get the word *optometry*, which has to do with literal eyesight.[10] From that, we can conclude that God appeared personally before Abram.

> Now the LORD had said to Abram: "Get out of your country, From your family And from your father's house, To a land that I will show you. I will make you a great nation; I will bless you And make your name great; And you shall be a blessing. I will bless those who bless you, And I will curse him who curses you; And in you all the families of the earth shall be blessed." (Genesis 12:1–3)

God later clarified the covenant and confirmed the promise was unconditional and required nothing on Abraham's part.

> On the same day the LORD made a covenant with Abram, saying: "To your descendants I have given this land, from the river of Egypt to the great river, the River Euphrates— the Kenites, the Kenezzites, the Kadmonites, the Hittites, the Perizzites, the Rephaim, the Amorites, the Canaanites, the Girgashites, and the Jebusites." (Genesis 15:18–21)

During the first 2000 years after creation, all were Gentiles. Then Abraham became the father of the Jewish race. His descendants (Israel) became God's chosen people. From the seed and earthly bloodline of Abraham would eventually come the Messiah. Throughout the Old Testament God commanded His people to remain a distinct and separate people and not to intermarry with Gentiles.

Years later God gave Moses the law for His people. From then until after Jesus came to earth, the Jews lived under the law.

The Law in the Gospels

Once I began studying the Word in depth, I started to understand what it really said as opposed to what I thought it would say. God opened my eyes to much that was new to me. Similarly, what you're about to read may be new to you.

When we understand the first four gospels, the rest of the Bible begins to make much better sense. Though it may seem hard to believe, the four gospels are an extension of the Old Testament—the Temple was still in place, and animals were still being sacrificed.

From the very beginning events in the gospels, we can clearly see that Jesus came to earth to fulfill God's covenant with Abraham and his descendants. Read what the angel Gabriel said to Mary:

> Then the angel said to her, "Do not be afraid, Mary, for you have found favor with God. And behold, you will conceive in your womb and bring forth a Son, and shall call His Name JESUS. He will be great, and will be called the Son of the Highest; and the Lord God will give Him the throne of His father David. And He will reign over the house of Jacob forever, and of His kingdom there will be no end." (Luke 1:30–33)

The term *throne of David* stems from the Old Testament. The *house of Jacob* refers to the kingdom. This is based on God's promises to Abraham, Isaac, and Jacob. The law was given to Moses. When David came on the scene, he was promised that his genealogy would produce the Messiah. This happened with the birth of Jesus.

Look further ahead in Luke 1 to verse 67. We meet Zacharias, the father of John the Baptist. Zacharias was an active temple priest working in Jerusalem when he was stricken so he could not speak during the pregnancy of his wife, Elizabeth. But at the time this Scripture passage was written, he was once again speaking, and the Jews understood that something supernatural was taking place.

> Now his father Zacharias was filled with the Holy Spirit, and prophesied, saying: Blessed *is* the Lord God of Israel, For He has visited and redeemed His people, And has raised up a horn of salvation for us In the house of His servant David, As He spoke by the mouth of His holy prophets, who *have been* since the world began, That we should be saved from our enemies And from the hand of all who hate us, To perform the mercy *promised* to our fathers And to remember His holy covenant, The oath which He swore to our father Abraham: To grant us that we, Being delivered from the hand of our enemies, Might serve Him without fear, In holiness and righteousness before Him all days of our life. (Luke 1:67–73)

This scripture tells us Zacharias "was filled with the Holy Spirit." When the Scripture speaks of someone being filled with the Holy Spirit, it means everything they speak is God-directed. God was speaking through Zacharias. Verse 68 makes it clear that He is the God of Israel: "for He hath visited and redeemed His people." He is talking to and about the nation of Israel. There is no mention of Gentiles in this verse. This verse is about David, who was Jewish and lived during Old Testament times. In David's time, they called on God to save them from their enemies. The Jews had the same enemies at the time John the Baptist was born, and they have the same enemies today.

Now let's return to the covenants and the oath made to Abraham. Genesis 12:1–3 predicted that one day Abraham's seed would become a great nation that would ultimately inherit the Promised Land. The glorious crowning seed of Abraham was his heir, Jesus of Nazareth, Jesus Christ, our Savior. Jesus came to earth to fulfill the law and prophecies. Jesus said this:

> "Do not think that I have come to abolish the Law or the Prophets; I have not come to abolish them but to fulfill them. For truly I tell you, until heaven and earth disappear, not the smallest letter, not the least stroke of a pen, will by any means disappear from the Law until everything is accomplished. Therefore anyone who sets aside one of the least of these commands and teaches others accordingly will be called least in the kingdom of heaven, but whoever practices and teaches these commands will be called great in the kingdom of heaven." (Matthew 5:17–19 NIV)

Jesus came to introduce Himself to Israel as their Messiah, their Redeemer, and their King. Yes, He came to shed His blood for the sins of all people—both Jews and Gentiles—but His appearance was to the nation of Israel, and at that point, the law was still in effect. Jesus Himself said, "I was not sent except to the lost sheep of the house of Israel" (Matthew 15:24).

Jesus gave His twelve disciples these instructions:

> These twelve Jesus sent out and commanded them, saying: "Do not go into the way of the Gentiles, and do not enter a city of the Samaritans. But go rather to the lost sheep of the house of Israel. And as you go, preach, saying, 'The kingdom of heaven is at hand.'" (Matthew 10:5–7)

Jesus didn't just *tell* His disciples—He *commanded* them not to go to the Gentiles or the Samaritans. Instead, they were "to go to the lost sheep of the house of Israel"— the Jewish race. The covenant with Abraham recorded in Genesis was with the house of Israel. Jesus came to fulfill the covenant, the law, and to fulfill ministry to the house of Israel.

During that time, Jesus' ministry to the twelve apostles was under the law. After healing the man with leprosy, He told him,

> "See that you tell no one; but go your way, show yourself to the priest, and offer the gift that Moses commanded, as a testimony to them." (Matthew 8:4)

Let me ask you this: When God gave Moses the law at Mt. Sinai, did He command him to share it with the Gentiles? No, the law was theirs and theirs alone. The apostles were sent to the "house of Israel," where they were to preach that the kingdom of heaven was at hand.

> From that time Jesus began to preach and to say, "Repent, for the kingdom of heaven is at hand." (Matthew 4:17)

I have used only a few of the many Scripture passages where Christ dealt with the law and with the Jews who lived under the law. The point here is that the four gospels describe Jesus' ministry to the Jewish people, the descendants of Abraham, and do not refer to the Body of Christ.

The kingdom of heaven Jesus was offering was not merely a spiritual kingdom; rather, He offered a real kingdom on earth. Not a form of government but a kingdom of change, nevertheless. It was at this time when Jesus was on earth that Israel was faced with the decision whether or not to accept Him as their king. The Jewish people were waiting for the kingdom on earth but believed the Messiah was coming to set up a government and deliver them from Roman rule. When Jesus returns, He will set up a government but that time had not yet come. Most of the Jews misunderstood the Scriptures—and missed their Messiah.

Jesus knew about the Body of Christ (the church). He knew the gospel was to be offered to the Gentiles as well as the Jews. But at that time He could not let His apostles know because the law had to be fulfilled to the very letter (Matthew 5:18). His loving heart was reaching out to the lost sheep of the house of Israel.

The book *Things to Come* by J. Dwight Pentecost includes an insert by Alva J. McClain:

> More than one expositor has stumbled over the ultimatum of Christ, "I was not sent but unto the lost sheep of the house of Israel." The only adequate explanation is to see what our Lord understood clearly, the contingent nature of His message of the kingdom. To put the matter in a

> word: *the immediate and complete establishment of His kingdom depended upon the attitude of the nation of Israel,* to whom pertained the divine promises and covenants.[11]

The Law After the Resurrection

As we read about the early church forming in the first chapters of Acts, we see that people who believed God for salvation and followed Christ did not shed their Jewish ways; instead, they continued to do everything the law demanded because they did not understand they were no longer under the law. Jesus had come to fulfill the law by offering us grace. We will see that revelation coming later through the apostle Paul. But first, we need to understand that the importance of Israel cannot be overstated. This truth carries through the Old Testament, the gospels, and on into the beginning chapters of Acts.

> When the Most High divided their inheritance to the nations, When He separated the sons of Adam, He set the boundaries of the peoples According to the number of the children of Israel. For the LORD's portion *is* His people; Jacob *is* the place of His inheritance. (Deuteronomy 32:8–9)

The Almighty God, the Creator of everything, in His sovereignty put the heavens and the earth in place and set the borders for every nation of people on the planet. Every nation's border was set "according to the number of the children of Israel."

When Peter preached in Solomon's Portico (Acts 2:17–24), he was preaching to the Jews, his brethren: "Yet now brethren." He reviewed what the prophets had foretold in the Old Testament. Peter urged his listeners to repent so Jesus would return and set up His physical kingdom on earth. In verse 24 Peter referred to "all the prophets from Samuel and those who follow"—those mentioned in the Old Testament and continuing through the New Testament. Peter continued during these early days after Christ's resurrection and ascension to speak to the Jews of Israel using such terms as "men of Israel," "the God of Abraham," and "God of our father."

> "You are sons of the prophets, and of the covenant which God made with our fathers, saying to Abraham, *'And in your seed all the families of the earth shall be blessed.'"* (Acts 3:25)

Peter was talking *to* the Jewish people, to Israel: "men of Judea." And he was talking *about* the Jewish people, the seed of Abraham. He was talking about the covenant God made with His people, Israel. Note the last part of the verse, *"All families of the earth shall be blessed."* Through the seed of Abraham would come the Messiah. Peter knew He had come, but His people had rejected Him.

Peter was talking to the first Jewish church.

The early Jewish believers taught that Jesus was crucified, rose from the grave, and then ascended to heaven. However, many of them also believed He would immediately return to set up His kingdom on earth and that they would shortly face the Great Tribulation. Because of their knowledge of the Old Testament, they knew these things would happen but mistakenly believed they would happen very soon. Later, Paul wrote a letter to explain that this was a false expectation.

The Jews who were saved after Jesus' resurrection received this message from the apostles: "He who believes and is baptized will be saved" (Mark 16:16).

We also find Peter preaching this:

> Then Peter said to them, "Repent, and let every one of you be baptized in the name of Jesus Christ for the remission of sins; and you shall receive the gift of the Holy Spirit." (Acts 2:38)

With few exceptions, the early church leadership was comprised of believing Jews. They preached basic truths like the gospel of the kingdom and the need to be baptized, but they added other rules like keeping the Ten Commandments and the necessity of male circumcision. Most of the Jews had already been circumcised according to the law, and they thought there was no way to be saved without also being circumcised.

The apostles were among the first to know about the death, burial, and resurrection once it became a reality, yet they too tried to live by the law and taught others to do likewise.

Remember, the disciples were still looking for Jesus to return and set up His kingdom on earth. The Old Testament prophets had written many Scripture passages about Israel and how the Jews would bring the light of salvation to the Gentiles. At that time, they had yet to hear a single prophecy that used the term *Body of Christ---as the church.*

These church leaders included people like James, the half brother of Jesus, and the apostle Peter. They would have known that in the book of Daniel, the Messiah was mentioned only in relation to the Jews. At that time, the disciples' main concern was preaching to the Jews; the mystery of how both Jews and Gentiles would be saved the same way remained a secret—until God finally gave the revelation to Paul. So how could they preach something they did not know?

Although they believed Jesus was the Son of God and salvation came through Him, they still felt compelled to continue their temple worship and to keep the Ten Commandments in order to be separate from the Gentiles.

A New Revelation: Law Fulfilled Through Grace

I mentioned earlier that the Bible is a progressive revelation. During the formation of the church, the apostles preached to the Jews and in large part continued ruling their lives by the law. Before the ascension, Jesus had told the apostles to preach to the whole world, but they failed to understand that this included the Gentiles. They still assumed they were to preach to the Jews. The twelve apostles, including Matthias, who had replaced Judas, went to every corner of the land where Jesus had visited, preaching in the synagogues, preaching to the Jews.

Then God brought a new man on the scene: Paul.

To our way of thinking, Paul was an unlikely candidate for the monumental task God set before him. Saul, as he was known until some point in his ministry, hated the followers of Christ. A highly educated man, he thought he knew the Scriptures. He was right and those people following Christ were wrong. Then when he was on the road to Damascus ready to persecute more believers, his entire world turned upside down. Jesus appeared to him.

> As he journeyed he came near Damascus, and suddenly a light shone around him from heaven. Then he fell to the ground, and heard a voice saying to him, "Saul, Saul, why are you persecuting Me?" And he said, "Who are You, Lord?" Then the Lord said, "I am Jesus, whom you are persecuting. It *is* hard for you to kick against the goads." So he, trembling and astonished, said, "Lord, what do You want me to do?" Then the Lord *said* to him, "Arise and go into the city, and you will be told what you must do." (Acts 9:3–6)

In a moment, Saul became a believer—a believer ready to give his life for his Savior, a believer ready to serve. "Lord, what do You want me to do?"

Temporarily blinded by the encounter, Saul was led to Damascus and waited for instructions. They came through a local believer named Ananias. Here is what God told Ananias about Saul:

> But the Lord said to him, "Go, for he is a chosen vessel of Mine to bear My name before Gentiles, kings, and the children of Israel. For I will show him How many things he must suffer for My name's sake." (Acts 9:15–16)

God ordained Paul to bring a new message, a new revelation from Jesus Christ.

> For I neither received it from man, nor was I

taught *it* but *it came* through the revelation of Jesus Christ. (Galatians 1:12)

To me, who am less than the least of all the saints, this grace was given, that I should preach among the Gentiles the unsearchable riches of Christ, and to make all see what *is* the fellowship of the mystery, which from the beginning of the ages has been hidden in God who created all things through Jesus Christ. (Ephesians 3:8–9)

A footnote in the NKJV about verse 9 says this: "Paul's mission as an apostle was to enlighten all people about the *mystery* of God's grace in Christ, which was not understood in previous times, but which had become clear with the coming of Jesus Christ."

The twelve Apostles were to be "witnesses" (Acts 1:22) of Christ's resurrection – that is, the fact of it. They were not to unfold fully the doctrine of it as Paul was. Just as God chose Moses to be revelator to Israel of all connected with the law dispensation; so God chose Saul of Tarsus to be the revelator and unfolder of the great body of doctrine for this age; those mighty truths connected with our Lord's death, burial, and resurrection, and His ascended Person. All the "mysteries" or "secrets" revealed to God's people in this dispensation by the Holy Ghost are revealed by Paul. Finally Paul is the unfolder of the great company of God's elect, called the Church, the Body of Christ, the individuals of which body are called members of the Body of Christ – members of Christ Himself.[12]

When persecution of followers of Christ began increasing, they scattered.

> Now those who were scattered after the persecution that arose over Stephen traveled as far as Phoenicia, Cyprus, and Antioch, preaching the word to no one but the Jews only. (Acts 11:19)

The Jews who were scattered went out and preached, but only to the Jews. Some eight years earlier, Jesus had told them to preach to all nations. However, they wanted to see the Jews saved right away because they still believed in a short time Jesus would return to establish His kingdom. The Jews who studied the Old Testament believed the covenant was for them—and it was. Their concern for the present was to take the message to the Jews first and then to the Gentiles.

> "I, the LORD, have called You in righteousness, And will hold Your hand; I will keep You and give You as a covenant to the people, As a light to the Gentiles." (Isaiah 42:6)

Peter especially did not want to break the law by preaching to Gentiles.

> "You know how unlawful it is for a Jewish man to keep company with or go to one of another nation." (Acts 10:28)

But God rocked his boat by sending him to a Gentile family. It wasn't long before he had to explain to his fellow evangelists that he had tried to resist the idea, but in the end, he had to obey the Lord, who had repeated the command to go three times (Acts 10:9–48). And Cornelius and many of his Gentile family and friends received Jesus.

Other apostles and brethren heard about Peter preaching to Gentiles and accused him of wrongdoing. But Peter defended what he had done. He explained how after the Gentiles believed, the Holy Spirit had fallen on them.

> "Then I remembered what the Lord had said: 'John baptized with water, but you will be baptized with the Holy Spirit.' So if God gave them the same gift he gave us who believed in the Lord Jesus Christ, who was I to think that I could stand in God's way?" (Acts 11:16–17 NIV)

His response seemed to satisfy them—at least for the time being.

> When they heard this, they had no further objections and praised God, saying, "So then, even to Gentiles God has granted repentance that leads to life." (Acts 11:18 NIV)

However, many of the believing Jews demanded that salvation required the new Christian Gentiles to keep the laws of Moses and to be circumcised. Most of the apostles were preaching one way of salvation, trying to hold on to the Jewish law, while Paul was preaching grace. Their messages may have been similar, but they were not the same. Over the years, confusion and even discord over the issue grew. Something had to be done.

> And certain *men* came down from Judea and taught the brethren, "Unless you are circumcised

> according to the custom of Moses, you cannot be saved." Therefore, when Paul and Barnabas had no small dissension and dispute with them, they determined that Paul and Barnabas and certain others of them should go up to Jerusalem, to the apostles and elders, about this question. (Acts 15:1–2)

And so the Jerusalem Council took place. "Now the apostles and elders came together to consider this matter" (Acts 15:6).

These men went to gather evidence that Paul failed to teach the law of Moses and that he didn't require those who were saved to be circumcised. As bizarre as it sounds, public bathhouses were popular then, making it easy to spy, trying to discover whether new believers were circumcised. It was clear to the accusers that this part of the Jewish custom was not being followed.

And it was not a small argument; it was a deeply divisive dispute. Should they preach only Christ, or should they preach Christ plus circumcision as well as the need to keep the Ten Commandments? The goal of the Jerusalem Council was to bring Paul and Barnabas in front of the elders, who were determined to straighten them out.

This was fourteen years after Paul's conversion. Up to that point, Paul and his followers were the only ones preaching regularly to both Jews and Gentiles. Most of the Jews wanted the Jewish converts to keep part of the Jewish laws. They still didn't see salvation as being through Christ alone; they still followed a self-concocted mixture of law and grace.

> But some of the sect of the Pharisees who believed
> rose up, saying, "It is necessary to circumcise
> them, and to command *them* to keep the law of
> Moses." (Acts 15:5)

Some Pharisees showed up at the meeting. Members of a religious and political party in Palestine in New Testament times, the Pharisees were convinced they knew more than others about the Jewish laws and what should be included in the gospel message. One distinctive feature of the Pharisees was their strong commitment to observe the law of God as it was interpreted and applied by the Old Testament scribes. They claimed the Jewish people could not know God's law and that only the Pharisees had the training to interpret for them. They strongly suggested that Paul keep the law. Thus, the stage was set for a fight.

Peter watched and listened. This was a formidable group of antagonists. Twelve years earlier God had used the salvation of Cornelius and his household to prepare Peter for this showdown with his fellow teachers. God always equips us for the battles ahead.

> And when there had been much dispute, Peter
> rose up and said to them: "Men *and* brethren, you
> know that a good while ago God chose among
> us, that by my mouth the Gentiles should hear
> the word of the gospel and believe. So God, who
> knows the heart, acknowledged them by giving
> them the Holy Spirit, just as *He did* to us." (Acts
> 15:7–8)

In my mind's eye, I can see Peter during this debate,

remembering how God had sent him to a Gentile (Cornelius) and then standing up to tell them that Gentiles could be saved just like the Jews. Peter acknowledged that they should all agree to preach the same gospel. The question was . . . which gospel should they preach?

> "But we believe that through the grace of the Lord Jesus Christ we shall be saved in the same manner as they." (Acts 15:11)

After hearing the case, the room became silent. Then James, the half brother of Jesus, spoke up.

> "Men *and* brethren, listen to me: Simon [Peter] has declared how God at the first visited the Gentiles to take out of them a people for His name. And with this the words of the prophets agree, just as it is written." (Acts 15:13–15)

Keep in mind that James was the spokesperson at this meeting. At this time, he apparently was one of the leaders, or maybe *the* leader. He quoted several verses from the Old Testament, including Amos 9:12, in which Amos prophesied that Israel would be restored, as well as all the Gentiles who are called by His name. After James spoke, they came to an agreement.

In the end, Peter convinced them by asking how they could demand that new believers follow laws that even the most faithful Jews could not keep. (See Acts 15:9–10.) Letters were then sent out to the churches to let them know that after eighteen years of disagreement, everyone would finally preach the same message—salvation by grace alone. It was also decided that Peter would preach to the Jews, and Paul would preach to the Gentiles.

Attendees included the apostles and delegates from the church at Jerusalem (Acts 15:1–29). The *Nelson's Student Bible Dictionary* calls this meeting of Paul and Barnabas with the apostles the Jerusalem Council.

> A conference was held in about AD 49 between delegates (including Paul and Barnabas) from the church at Antioch of Syria and delegates from the church at Jerusalem. This council met to settle a dispute over whether Gentile converts to Christianity first had to identify with Judaism by being circumcised (Acts 15:1–29).

The dictionary goes on to say this:

> The conclusion of the Jerusalem Council, which determined that Gentiles did not have to be circumcised, was a sweeping victory for Paul. Speaking for the council, the apostle Peter declared:
>
> But we believe that through the grace of the Lord Jesus Christ we shall be saved in the same manner as they (Acts 15:11).
>
> The Jerusalem Council decreed, therefore, that the Gentiles should make four reasonable concessions of their own: We write to them to abstain from things polluted by idols, from sexual immorality, from things strangled, and from blood (Acts 15:20–29; 21:25).[13]

The time mentioned in the dictionary confirms that this meeting took place around eighteen years after Jesus ascended. We know from Acts 15:1 that many wanted to bring the new Gentile believers under the rule of the Mosaic Law. However, the apostle Paul was their champion, preaching that grace meant salvation without the need to keep the law. Now, for the very first time they all agreed. The law does not save. Both Jews and Gentiles are saved by grace through faith in our risen Savior, Jesus Christ.

Peter was deeply steeped in Judaism, even after the Jerusalem Council where they all agreed to preach the same gospel. It was hard for him to accept that the law is merely our tutor. Paul explained it this way:

> Therefore the law was our tutor *to bring us* to Christ, that we might be justified by faith. But after faith has come, we are no longer under a tutor. (Galatians 3:24–25)

In fact, when Peter went to Antioch, he separated himself from the Gentiles and joined the Jews who were strictly observing the Jewish law. Paul stood up to Peter and the others for playing the "hypocrite" and told him "they were not straightforward about the truth of the gospel" (Galatians 2:11–16).

It is believed Peter was coming to the end of his life as he wrote his second letter, and he had read all of Paul's letters. Read these last four verses of his epistle:

> Consider *that* the longsuffering of our Lord *is* salvation—as also our beloved brother Paul,

according to the wisdom given to him, has written to you, as also in all his epistles, speaking in them of these things, in which are some things hard to understand, which untaught and unstable *people* twist to their own destruction, as *they do* also the rest of the Scriptures. You therefore, beloved, since you know *this* beforehand, beware lest you also fall from your own steadfastness, being led away with the error of the wicked; but grow in the grace and knowledge of our Lord and Savior Jesus Christ. To Him *be* the glory both now and forever. Amen. (2 Peter 3:15–18)

Peter admitted that many things were hard for even him to understand, and he warned us that people would try to change the Scriptures to fit their needs and desires. People who have knowledge of the Bible but have lost their way sometimes twist words or take them out of context to fit their own beliefs, veering away from the truth. Peter tells us to study God's Word and not allow ourselves to be led astray by false teaching. I suspect that, although he had a hard time understanding Paul's mysteries about the Body of Christ and the rapture, he put his stamp of approval on Paul's epistles, confirming they were to be trusted just as much as the rest of the Bible.

For by grace you have been saved through faith, and that not of yourselves; *it is* the gift of God, not of works, lest anyone should boast. (Ephesians 2:8–9)

chapter 7
Birth of the Church

What is the church?

The church, the Body of Christ, is made up of the followers of Jesus Christ. It is not a denomination. It is not limited to a building. It is made up of Christian believers— past, present, and future.

The Birth of the Church

After Jesus Christ rose from the grave, He remained on earth for forty days to show He was alive and give some final encouragement and instruction to His followers. Many people witnessed Jesus after His resurrection, and then the apostles watched Him rise into the clouds from the Mount of Olives.

Before ascending to heaven, Jesus gave specific instructions to the followers who were with Him.

> And being assembled together with *them,* He commanded them not to depart from Jerusalem, but to wait for the Promise of the

Father, "which," *He said,* "you have heard from
Me; for John truly baptized with water, but you
shall be baptized with the Holy Spirit not many
days from now." Therefore, when they had come
together, they asked Him, saying, "Lord, will You
at this time restore the kingdom to Israel?" And
He said to them, "It is not for you to know times
or seasons which the Father has put in His own
authority. But you shall receive power when the
Holy Spirit has come upon you; and you shall be
witnesses to Me in Jerusalem, and in all Judea
and Samaria, and to the end of the earth." (Acts
1:4–8)

The people gathered there must have been in awe. Can't
you see them standing there, staring into the sky with mouths
hanging open in wonder?

Now when He had spoken these things, while
they watched, He was taken up, and a cloud
received Him out of their sight. And while they
looked steadfastly toward heaven as He went up,
behold, two men stood by them in white apparel,
who also said, "Men of Galilee, why do you stand
gazing up into heaven? This *same* Jesus, who was
taken up from you into heaven, will so come in
like manner as you saw Him go into heaven."
(Acts 1:9–11)

And so they pulled themselves together and returned to
Jerusalem to wait for the Promise.

Then they returned to Jerusalem from the mount
called Olivet, which is near Jerusalem, a Sabbath

day's journey. And when they had entered, they went up into the upper room where they were staying: Peter, James, John, and Andrew; Philip and Thomas; Bartholomew and Matthew; James *the son* of Alphaeus and Simon the Zealot; and Judas *the son* of James. These all continued with one accord in prayer and supplication, with the women and Mary the mother of Jesus, and with His brothers. (Acts 1:12–14)

Reading further, we learn that about 120 people were gathered in that room. And then on the day of Pentecost (fifty days after Passover) it happened. Jesus, as He had promised, baptized them with the Holy Spirit.

When the Day of Pentecost had fully come, they were all with one accord in one place. And suddenly there came a sound from heaven, as of a rushing mighty wind, and it filled the whole house where they were sitting. Then there appeared to them divided tongues, as of fire, and *one* sat upon each of them. And they were all filled with the Holy Spirit and began to speak with other tongues, as the Spirit gave them utterance. (Acts 2:1–4)

Jesus said they would receive power to witness. And they did. Peter began using this new power as he preached that very day. As a result, about three thousand souls were saved (Acts 2:41), and the church was born.

In the Beginning: A Jewish Church

In the beginning, the church was made up of many more Jews than Gentiles. As explained in the previous chapter, the apostles focused on preaching to the Jews. In fact, there was a wall of separation between the Jews and Gentiles—a wall that could only come down through the grace and peace Jesus brought.

> For He Himself is our peace, who has made both one, and has broken down the middle wall of separation. (Ephesians 2:14)

An NKJV footnote comments on this verse.

> **The middle wall of separation** between Jews and Gentiles was vividly portrayed by an actual partition in the temple area, with a sign warning that any Gentile going beyond the Court of the Gentiles would receive swift and sudden death.

Most everything before the cross concerned the Jewish law. During the early days of the church, the apostles, as we learned in Chapter 6, were still guided in large part by the law. And because of this, they either refused or were reluctant to offer the gospel to Gentiles. As we learned, God moved first through Peter, and then more fully through Paul, to bring a greater understanding of grace, grace for everyone—both Jew and Gentile.

The Gentiles Are Recognized as Joint Heirs

Paul continued what had started the day of Pentecost, but the church began to move more fully into the dispensation of grace with his salvation and commissioning. God worked through him to give Jews and Gentiles equal status in the church. Read what Paul wrote to the church at Ephesus:

> If indeed you have heard of the dispensation of the grace of God which was given to me for you, how that by revelation He made known to me the mystery (as I have briefly written already, by which, when you read, you may understand my knowledge in the mystery of Christ), which in other ages was not made known to the sons of men, as it has now been revealed by the Spirit to His holy apostles and prophets: that the Gentiles should be fellow heirs, of the same body and partakers of His promise in Christ through the gospel, of which I became a minister according to the gift of the grace of God given to me by the effective working of His power. (Ephesians 3:2–7)

The dispensation of grace was given to Paul for everyone. God revealed this truth to him, and Peter most likely learned from him. God also gave Peter the visions described in Acts 10 and sent him to the Gentile household of Cornelius to begin opening his eyes to salvation through Christ being open to Gentiles as well as Jews. Even though believers were first called Christians at the church Paul served in Antioch, a church made up of both Jews and Gentiles, Peter and the other apostles did not see things yet quite as Paul did.

In the beginning, Peter and Paul preached different gospels. The apostles were preaching the gospel of the kingdom and still saw themselves under law more than grace. The Jerusalem Council where the Jewish leaders finally conceded that the gospel should be made available to Gentiles as well as Jews took place at least eighteen years after Jesus' ascension. What were the apostles teaching during that time?

> But some of the sect of the Pharisees who believed rose up, saying, "It is necessary to circumcise them, and command *them* to keep the law of Moses." (Acts 15:5)

These were not the religious Pharisees. They were believing Pharisees, followers of Christ. Yet they were using strong words like *command*. That was what they understood: God/Moses/Law/Israel. Paul was teaching the gospel of grace: God/Paul/Grace/Gentiles-Jews. They agreed to Paul's teaching only after the Jerusalem Council.

The Jewish believers thought Jesus would come back soon and were looking for Him to return while they were still alive. They walked, talked with, and lived with Jesus for three years and saw that He always kept the law. After He was crucified, many years elapsed before they could fully accept the gospel of Jesus Christ given to Paul.

> Moreover, brethren, I declare to you the gospel which I preached to you, which also you received and in which you stand, by which also you are saved, if you hold fast that word which I preached to you---unless you believed in vain. For I delivered to you first of all that which I also

received: that Christ died for our sins according
to the Scriptures, and that He was buried, and
that He rose again the third day according to the
Scriptures. (1 Corinthians 15:1–4)

Paul's gospel came after the cross. He continually discusses
the importance of the death, burial, and resurrection of our
risen Savior and His blood shed for our sins. Paul tells us to
preach about Christ crucified on the cross. This is offensive
to most Jews and nonsense to many Gentiles.

For Jews request a sign, and Greeks [Gentiles] seek
after wisdom; but we preach Christ crucified, to
the Jews a stumbling block and to the Greeks
foolishness. (1 Corinthians 1:22–23)

He goes on to say that the power of God's salvation is
for both the Jews and the Gentiles. Paul was not taught by
man—he learned from Jesus Christ.

For I neither received it from man, nor was I
taught *it*, but *it came* through the revelation of
Jesus Christ. (Galatians 1:12)

God chose Paul to bring His message to everyone. Here
is what He told Ananias when He sent him to the newly save
Saul, who became known as Paul:

The Lord said to Ananias, "Go, for he is a chosen
vessel of Mine to bear My name before Gentiles,
kings, and the children of Israel." (Acts 9:15)

Jesus Christ revealed to Paul that the law had no power

to save. It is useful only to show us what sin is. The first four gospels cover the birth, death, and resurrection of Jesus, during which Jesus fulfilled the law. Paul taught salvation by grace through faith.

> *There is* therefore now no condemnation to those who are in Christ Jesus, who do not walk according to the flesh, but according to the Spirit. For the law of the Spirit of life in Christ Jesus has made me free from the law of sin and death. (Romans 8:1–2)

Paul's letters written to the churches of his time are also for the church today. We learn in those letters that we are saved by grace through faith, a gift from God. We cannot add any works, laws, or rituals. If we add anything, we deny the sufficiency of Christ's death, burial, and resurrection for our salvation.

> But now the righteousness of God apart from the law is revealed, being witnessed by the Law and the Prophets, even the righteousness of God, through faith in Jesus Christ, to all and on all who believe. For there is no difference; for all have sinned and fall short of the glory of God, being justified freely by His grace through the redemption that is in Christ Jesus, whom God set forth *as* a propitiation by His blood, through faith, to demonstrate His righteousness, because in His forbearance God had passed over the sins that were previously committed, to demonstrate at the present time His righteousness, that He might be just and the justifier of the one who has faith in Jesus. (Romans 3:21–26)

The Pauline letters give us a clear picture of this salvation by grace through faith. The Scriptures record that Jesus gave the gospel to Paul and instructed him that it was for "the Jew first and also for the Greek [Gentile]."

> For I am not ashamed of the gospel of Christ, for it is the power of God to salvation for everyone who believes, for the Jew first and also for the Greek. (Romans 1:16)

The Church's Responsibility to Israel

Jesus died for everyone—both Jew and Gentile. He loves each person unconditionally—both Jew and Gentile. That is why He gave His life for us. However, He also has a special role for Gentiles to play in the lives of His chosen people, Israel. Part of that role is to provoke them to jealousy so they too will receive salvation through their faith in Christ (Romans 11:11).

> For I do not desire, brethren, that you should be ignorant of this mystery, lest you should be wise in your own opinion, that blindness in part has happened to Israel until the fullness of the Gentiles has come in. (Romans 11:25)

That blindness will last only until "the fullness of the Gentiles has come in." It has been about two thousand years now. Only God knows when the time will come for Jesus Christ to bring the Body of Christ to Him.

All this is in God's plan. Paul is making the point that through the Jews' rejection, salvation has come to the

Gentiles. This should make us want to witness and plant the seeds to the Jewish race as we continue to share the gospel with everyone who desires to listen. It was the Jewish race that first brought the gospel to the Gentiles. We need to share the gospel with them and the world.

chapter 8

The Church Today

Through the years, the church has gone through many changes—and still is. After centuries of struggle and change, Christianity and Judaism finally emerged as two separate walks of faith. For many centuries now, we have experienced the Day of the Gentiles.

The Apostle's Creed was first formed in the second century and eventually evolved into its final form in the eighth century. Through the ages, theological disagreements led to conflict among believers. We saw the rise of the Roman Catholic Church, the Crusades, the emergence of Protestantism, and the development of many creeds and denominations.

What about today? In the United States, we hear our president give a state of the union address every year. But what is the state of the church?

A study of prophetic scripture can help us understand what has been, what is, and what is yet to come. We are touching some highlights in this book, but I encourage you to commit to additional Bible study. One I would recommend is *Through the Bible* with Les Feldick (www.lesfeldick.org).

†

> But know this, that in the last days perilous times will come: For men will be lovers of themselves, lovers of money, boasters, proud, blasphemers, disobedient to parents, unthankful, unholy, unloving, unforgiving, slanderers, without self-control, brutal, despisers of good, traitors, headstrong, haughty, lovers of pleasure rather than lovers of God, having a form of godliness but denying its power. And from such people turn away! (2 Timothy 3:1–5)

Hmmm. Sound familiar? Sadly, as we look around we can see many people—some of them in the church—fitting this description.

Apostasy

Apostasy is the falling away from faith. One of the definitions in Webster's is "abandonment of a previous affection; defection."

Apostasy has been around a long time. Paul, Peter, Jude, John, Titus, and James (the half brother of Jesus) warned us about the falling away from faith. The problem of apostasy crept in soon after Paul started his churches, and he wasted no time in writing to these churches to address it. Later, toward the end of Peter's and John's lives, they also gave warnings about falling away. Jude wrote only one chapter and it is about apostasy.

The church in the United States has conformed to the world in so many ways. From 1940 to 1960, the number of Christian churches and believing Christians was on the rise in the United States. However, since 1960, Christian faith in our country has slowly deteriorated. Less than 24 years after World War II, Europe and the United States began to fall under the crush of that era of drugs, sex, and rock festivals where participants indulged freely in sex and drugs. The sixties brought marijuana, heroin, and cocaine. This deterioration of moral standards threatened the moral structure of the church.

Churches and seminaries have become more liberal, wanting to appease and tolerate. Many people no longer consider homosexuality a sin. During the last twenty years, the weakening of faith has accelerated. Many who once held to the faith based on God's Word are sliding from the faith or are more tolerant of other beliefs and unbiblical behaviors than they were. Some even contradict God's Word. In a 2011 study by the Barna Group analyzing changes in believers since 1991, some issues had improved, but many had declined. Shockingly, one of the sharpest declines was in the number of people believing in the accuracy of the Bible.

> The largest change in beliefs was the ten-point decline in those who firmly believe that the Bible is accurate in all of the principles it teaches. Only 43% of self-identified Christians now have such a strong belief in the Bible.[14]

God knew this time would come—nothing takes Him by surprise. In the book of Revelation, the apostle John recorded messages from Christ to seven churches. These seven churches represent specific time periods, and each message reveals a lesson for us today.

The Seven Churches

The following notes on the *commendations, criticisms, instructions,* and *promises* found in these messages to the churches are from the NKJV.

The first church was called Ephesus (Revelation 2:1–7), and it spoke to the time from AD 32 to AD 132, overlapping the message to Smyrna from AD 64 To AD 132. The *commendation* was for rejecting evil, persevering, and having patience. The *criticism* was that they had left their first love of Christ. The *instruction* was to do the works they did at first and the *promise* to eat from the Tree of Life.

The second church was Smyrna (Revelation 2:8–11), and it dealt with the years from AD 64 to AD 312. The *commendation* was for gracefully bearing suffering. There was no *criticism*. The *instruction* was to "be faithful until death" and the *promise* the crown of life. Revelation 2:9 references the "synagogue of Satan." Some scholars have stated the synagogue of Satan always reflects the idea that the church has replaced Israel. This would be about the time Replacement Theology started. This theology is in error but is growing in churches in our day.

The third church was called Pergamos (Revelation 2:12–17), and it was tied to the years from AD 312 to AD 606. The *commendation* was that they were keeping the faith of Christ and the *criticism* that they tolerated immorality, idolatry, and heresies. The *instruction* was to repent and the *promise* hidden manna and a stone with a new name. What did the true Christian church have to change or believe? It had to let amillennialism replace pre-millennialism. Christians were taught not to read the Scriptures for themselves but to rely on the priest to interpret for them. These changes were done deliberately to create a church-state religion. History records that the developments took place during that time.

For the years from AD 606 to AD 1517 we look at the fourth church, Thyatira (Revelation 2:18–29). The *commendation* was that their love, service, faith, and patience were greater than at first, and the *criticism* that they tolerated immorality, idolatry, and heresies. The *instruction* cautioned them that judgment was coming and to keep the faith. The *promise* was that they would rule over nations and receive the morning star. During this time, Mass began with the priest blessing the wafer in prayer to God and Mary. Today many think the transmuted communion will impart a grace that forgives some sins. These practices are confirmed in our historical records of those years.

The fifth church, Sardis (Revelation 3:1–6), was from AD 1517 to AD 1750. The *commendation* was that some had kept the faith and the *criticism* that they were a dead church. The *instruction* was to repent and strengthen what remained, and the *promise* was the faithful honored and clothed in white. The reformation churches came in that era and initiated reform to remove idols and other forms of evil. Martin Luther nailed *The Ninety-five Theses* to the door of the Wittenberg Castle in Germany. Men like Tyndale published Bibles so anyone able to read could understand God's Word. John Knox surfaced as the great reformer of Scotland. Augustinian Calvinism taught true Christians are chosen by God, that their destiny was set and no one, including the pope, could change that. They kept the doctrine of amillennialism and their belief in Replacement Theology. History confirms these details. It would be another 200 years before the Great Awakening.

The sixth church was Philadelphia (Revelation 3:7–13) from AD 1750 to AD 1948. They overlapped a short time with Laodicea. The *commendation* was that they persevered in the faith, kept the word of Christ, and honored His name. There was no *criticism*. Their *instruction* was to keep the faith, and their *promise* included a place in God's presence, a new name, and the New Jerusalem. This is a period of missionary activity. Some of our greatest Bible scholars wrote books and were able to interpret scriptures not understood before. This era gave us many great scholars: John Nelson Darby, C. I. Scofield, A. C. Dixon, E. W. Bullinger, Charles H. Spurgeon, and Robert Anderson. Thousands of years ago, God said this to Daniel: "Go *your way*, Daniel, for the words *are* closed up and sealed till the time of the end" (Daniel 12:9). We are coming closer to the end, and God is opening the Scriptures not previously understood. Billy Sunday, Billy Graham, and J. Dwight Pentecost contributed greatly. The Great Awakening began. (How long would it last? It began to fade away in the 1960s. Now in 2013, it does not look like it will return. It would take God's people, the believers who make up the church, to turn things around. But at present, the church is sliding just as God said it would in the end). Many during this time recognized pre-millennialism and rejected Calvinism in favor of true missionary activity.

We saw the reestablishment of the nation of Israel. The eyes of anyone who thought the church had replaced Israel should have been opened when they saw Israel's restoration in 1948. They should have left the Synagogue of Satan, also called Replacement Theology, and cried out to God for His salvation. Again, all this is confirmed by historical records. We now move to the last church.

The seventh and last church, Laodicea, covers 1948 until the rapture of the church. You read correctly. We are in the last church age Jesus revealed to us through John.

The church is called Laodicea (Revelation 3:14–22). The *commendation*? None. *Criticism:* indifferent. The *instruction* is to be zealous and repent, and the *promise* is to share Christ's throne.

Lessons from Laodicea

Laodicea was on a seacoast and was part of a major trade route. This was a wealthy town and the people assumed they needed no help from anybody. It was reported they had an earthquake around AD 17, but they told Rome they did not need financial help. The one thing they needed was water—they had to go a great distance to get it. They made pipes and brought the water into their town. The water had a mineral taste and since the pipes were above ground, the water came into town lukewarm. The people in Laodicea did not enjoy the lukewarm, mineral-flavored water and must have spit it out at times. They knew what Jesus was talking about when He said, "So then, because you are lukewarm, and neither cold nor hot, I will vomit you out of My mouth" (Revelation 3:16).

Paul was concerned about the church in Laodicea when he wrote a letter to the church in Colosse, about eleven miles away. The two churches were to share their letters from Paul (see Colossians 4:16). In Colossians 2:1–10 Paul reminded them they could understand the mystery of God. What did they do? They were taken in by philosophy and teaching that did not conform to a proper knowledge of God.

What are the vast majority doing today? Following the same pattern, people today, especially in the United States, believe they can fix everything. That most if not all teaching is as good as the Bible. Yes, we are in the last days even though many will scoff and make fun if you say such a thing. Peter told us this would happen in the last days.

> Knowing this first: that scoffers will come in the last days, walking according to their own lusts, and saying, "Where is the promise of His coming? For since the fathers fell asleep, all things continue as *they were* from the beginning of creation." (2 Peter 3:3–4)

> Therefore do not cast away your confidence, which has great reward. For you have need of endurance, so that after you have done the will of God, you may receive the promise: *"For yet a little while, And He who is coming will come and will not tarry."* (Hebrews10:35–37)

Don't ever doubt it. He is coming when it is time for Him to come, and nothing will prevent it.

Me-Focus Replaces God-Focus

Apostasy should always be a concern for us as it can creep into a church so easily. The church that welcomes everybody's ideals, rather than following Scripture, is an easy place for apostasy to start. We see the breakdown of morals in churches today. Many have stated that homosexuality is not a sin. Some even allow homosexuals to be clergy. Name-it-and-claim-it and feel-good churches are popular. Countless Christians are trapped in the snare of pornography and adulterous relationships. And on and on . . .

People are becoming more and more self-focused. Many ministries turn their followers' focus to "me" instead of God. *God can do this for me. I am expecting God to do that.* Instead of focusing on loving and serving Him, we become engrossed in the blessings He offers us. Yes, He does offer blessings. But we are to seek Him first. Always.

> "But seek first the kingdom of God and His righteousness, and all these things shall be added to you." (Matthew 6:33)

> Trust in the LORD with all your heart, And lean not on your own understanding; In all your ways acknowledge Him, And He shall direct your paths. (Proverbs 3:5–6)

Satan is making a sweep around the world with the apostasies of the church. We need to be obedient to Christ and speak out against false teaching.

Emergent Churches

Today we hear about the growing number of emergent churches. In my view, an emergent church is one that has moved from the conservative strong biblical faith to a liberal faith because congregants feel it fits better into their community. Emergent churches seek common ground with other religions. Are they leading the way to the one-world church prophesied for the end times?

From my studies, I have identified the following characteristics of an emergent church.

- Members and leadership think there is no need to study Bible prophecies because they are too hard to understand.

- Israel is less and less important. The church and Israel are equal, or the church is fulfilling the promises for Israel.

- Bible study is being replaced by studying books and methods (man's ideas).

- Church health is evaluated only by the number of people who attend.

- The study of the truth in God's Word becomes less important.

- People don't bring their Bibles to church.

- God's Word—especially concepts like hell, lake of fire, sin, and repentance—is downplayed to prevent offending anyone.

- Political correctness is more important and safer than taking on adversity and being bold in teaching and living God's Word.

In emergent or weakening churches, hired shepherds will often back away when trouble starts because they do not like hardships. Godly shepherds should take complete responsibility for their sheep and meet adversity head-on, depending on God.

Counterfeits

People across our land are on a spiritual search. But far too many are finding answers in the wrong places.

What do we see today? We have New Age groups that worship almost everything but the true God. They talk about oneness with God as though God is in trees and in everything. Our public schools even have Earth Day, a form of worship the New Age adherents use to worship trees and Mother Earth.

> The New Age (NAM) movement has many sub-divisions, but it is generally a collection of Eastern-influenced metaphysical thought systems, a conglomeration of theologies, hopes, and expectations held together with an eclectic teaching of salvation, of "correct thinking," and "correct knowledge." It is a theology of "feel-goodism," "universal tolerance," and "moral relativism. . . . It is supposed to bring in peace and enlightenment and reunite man with God. Man is presently considered separated from God not because of sin (Isaiah 59:2), but because of lack of understanding and knowledge concerning the true nature of God and reality."[15]

The New Age movement is a counterfeit movement that reaches worldwide, like a New Age spiritual revival. This type of Eastern mystical belief has infiltrated the world.

New Agers may think they have found the answer, but they are missing it. People look to other cults and religions. But they are missing it too. Jesus Christ is the only answer. He is the only way to true and lasting peace, forgiveness, and eternal life.

> Jesus told him, "I am the way, the truth, and the life. No one can come to the Father except through me." (John 14:6 NLT)

The Church at Laodicea

In one of John's visions described in Revelation, he sees Jesus addressing seven churches. One was the church at Laodicea. This is part of His message:

> "'These things says the Amen, the Faithful and True Witness, the Beginning of the creation of God: "I know your works, that you are neither cold nor hot. I could wish you were cold or hot. So then, because you are lukewarm, and neither cold nor hot, I will vomit you out of My mouth. Because you say, 'I am rich, have become wealthy, and have need of nothing'—and do not know that you are wretched, miserable, poor, blind, and naked.""" (Revelation 3:14–17)

Does this describe the church in America today? Have we abandoned our first love? Have we defected? Have we allowed ourselves to get lazy? To be molded by the norms of society? God's Word warns against this.

> I beseech you therefore, brethren, by the mercies of God, that you present your bodies a living sacrifice, holy, acceptable to God, *which is* your reasonable service. And do not be conformed to this world, but be transformed by the renewing of your mind, that you may prove what *is* that good and acceptable and perfect will of God. (Romans 12:1–2)

Many churches try to blend into their community's culture and to please all religious beliefs. But we are not to conform. We are not to compromise. And we are certainly not to stay lukewarm or hover in our comfort zone. We are to seek God first—as a church and as individuals. We need to return to our first love, praising and expressing our gratitude to Him. Only then will we please Him. And only then can we make a difference.

Take a Stand

There was a dark age when the Bible became a forbidden book. Then reformers came to the forefront. Bibles were printed and translated into various languages and people began to study. The light of God arose through the gospel and many came to know Jesus Christ as Savior.

In many places, the Bible is outlawed. *Yes, in those countries that persecute Christians* you may think. *That could never happen here.* But look around the United States at what is happening.

Christians are being denied their freedom of expression. And it is getting worse. Just follow the work of Christian organizations like Liberty Counsel (http://www.lc.org) or The American Center for Law and Justice (ACLJ) (http://aclj.org). You may be shocked to learn how fast our freedom is shrinking.

Satan is the prince of this world (Job 2:2; John 12:31; 14:30; 16:11; Ephesians 2:2; 2 Corinthians 4:4). Satan first deceived Eve in the garden of Eden. He is the deceiver in heaven and earth. He deceived many angels who fell with him, and he is deceiving churches and individual believers today as well.

Our country has made a 180-degree turn. Universities that once required students to have a strong biblical education now ridicule them if they say Jesus is the only way to heaven or the Bible is the inspired Word of God. We are killing babies. More than 55 million abortions have taken place in the United States since Roe v. Wade in 1973.[16] Same-sex marriage is now legal in a growing number of states. The U.S. government is getting more powerful while most of its citizens are getting poorer. The government is starting to control us like servants. The main news media have prostituted themselves and joined the group that favors socialism.

Have we seen any of our government leaders who represent us bowing down to people who do not believe? I heard President Barack Hussein Obama on TV—while overseas talking directly to Muslims and the world—say the United States is not a Christian nation. He seemed to be bragging about it. It sent chill bumps down my spine.

It seems to me that bowing down and trying to appease our enemy is watering down our faith in God. We have seen past presidents try to please other nations by putting pressure on Israel. But God promises to bless those who bless Israel and curse those who curse Israel (Genesis 12:3).

Who is to blame? We all are when we let our nation—which was founded on biblical beliefs—slip away because we have not stood up to the ones who are taking God out of our lives. Many people should be speaking out, but they are not. Change must begin in the church.

> "If My people who are called by My name will humble themselves, and pray and seek My face, and turn from their wicked ways, then I will hear from heaven, and will forgive their sin and heal their land." (2 Chronicles 7:14)

As we see in prophecy, nothing surprises God. Bible prophecies show clearly that we are nearing the end times. I believe the Day of the Lord is close.

What Can We Do?

First, get ourselves right with God. Have you ever received Him as your Lord and Savior? If not, you can do that right now. If you admit you have sinned and need forgiveness. If you believe Jesus is the Son of God and died on the cross for your sins. If you are ready to follow Him . . . just tell Him right now. He is waiting for you with open arms.

> We are made right with God by placing our faith

in Jesus Christ. And this is true for everyone who believes, no matter who we are. For everyone has sinned; we all fall short of God's glorious standard. Yet God, with undeserved kindness, declares that we are righteous. He did this through Christ Jesus when he freed us from the penalty for our sins. For God presented Jesus as the sacrifice for sin. People are made right with God when they believe that Jesus sacrificed his life, shedding his blood. (Romans 3:22–25 NLT)

If you are a Christian, have you lost your first love? Are you living a lukewarm faith? Are you being conformed to the world? I encourage you to get down on your knees and ask God to show you everything in your life that needs to change. And then seek His will. He has a plan for you. He wants you to make a difference. And He will provide whatever you need to accomplish His purpose for you. All you need to do is say yes—and follow Him.

We should be burdened to tell more people how to get to heaven, and we should pray for and support Israel.

God wants us to continue to pray for one another, our country, and our leaders. But don't compromise your faith. Be willing to speak out. Be willing to take a stand.

And share the good news of Jesus Christ! He is our only hope. He is our only answer.

chapter 9
Israel Today

To the Jews First . . . and Then the Gentiles

Although Jesus came to earth to die for everyone—Jew and Gentile alike—He first brought the message to the Jews. And He told His disciples to go to the Jews.

> These twelve Jesus sent out and commanded them, saying: "Do not go into the way of the Gentiles, and do not enter a city of the Samaritans. But go rather to the lost sheep of the house of Israel." (Matthew 10:5–6)

Although He did heal the Canaanite woman's daughter, He first said this to the woman:

> But He answered and said, "I was not sent except to the lost sheep of the house of Israel." (Matthew 15:24)

Even Paul started out preaching to the Jews first. He customarily went to the synagogues where the Jews met. He tried to preach to the Jews in Corinth about Jesus being their Messiah and Savior, but received such opposition from them that he determined to go to the Gentiles.

> But when they opposed him and blasphemed, he
> shook *his* garments and said to them, "Your blood
> *be* upon your *own* heads; I *am* clean. From now on
> I will go to the Gentiles." (Acts 18:6)

Many Jews have continued—until this day—to reject Jesus as their long-awaited Messiah.

The Time of the Gentiles Will End

The Jews had enjoyed being a "special treasure" and blessing from God (see Psalm 135:4), but they lost their advantage through sin and unfaithfulness to God. With so many unbelieving Jews, the Gentile believers in the church grew to outnumber the Jews who followed Christ, and the time of the Gentiles was ushered in.

Because of their unfaithfulness and refusal to believe Jesus was their Messiah, for almost two thousand years, most of Israel has been blind to the gospel message. Some have come to faith—many Messianic congregations have formed—but most of the Jewish people are still spiritually blind to the truth about Jesus. However, Paul made it clear that this time of blindness would end—when "the fullness of the Gentiles has come in."

> For I do not desire, brethren, that you should
> be ignorant of this mystery, lest you should be
> wise in your own opinion, that blindness in part

has happened to Israel until the fullness of the Gentiles has come in. And so all Israel will be saved, as it is written: *"The Deliverer will come out of Zion, And He will turn away ungodliness from Jacob; For this is My covenant with them, When I take away their sins."* (Romans 11:25–27)

Yes, the time is coming when their eyes will be open and "all Israel will be saved."

Jesus Is the Only Way—for Both Jews and Gentiles

God has given me a great love for Jewish people. Most of them still do not believe the truth of saving grace through Yeshua (Jesus). They do not understand that the Ten Commandments and other laws are not the way to salvation. The law is our teacher—shows us that we cannot earn our way to heaven through obedience because all of us sin. The Bible clearly shows that Jesus, Yeshua, Messiah is the only way. Whether Jew or Gentile, we can find forgiveness and salvation only through Him.

I talked to Rose Price, a survivor of the Holocaust, which brutally took the lives of six million Jews. She was doing a TV taping at *Jewish Voice*. She talked about how the Nazis took her from her home at age eleven. Later, when she was twelve, German guards beat her unmercifully with a rod. She said her family first thought the Germans were going to help them because the Jews thought the Germans were Christians. However, her family was told (and believed) that they were being killed because they were Christ killers.

Sharing Christ with Jewish People

Witnessing to a Jew is not much different from witnessing to a Gentile. How should you do it? First, prayerfully. Let them see Christ in the way you live. Love them with His love. And be sensitive. Help them understand that when they accept Jesus as Messiah, they remain a Jew. They do not have to leave culture and tradition behind. But they need to know they are saved by grace, not by works.

Be wise in your conversation.

- The phrase "convert to Christianity" can block their minds and set off a red flag so they cannot hear anything else you say.

- Focus on having a relationship with Yeshua (Jesus).

- *Yeshua* is the Hebrew word for Jesus. It means salvation. Instead of the word *Christ*, use *Messiah,* which means the *Anointed One.*

- Jews think of Christianity and church as another religion. Therefore, instead of using the word *Christian,* use the term *believer* or *follower of Yeshua.*

- The word *cross* is so meaningful to Christians, but to the Jews it brings the memory of Nazi soldiers who were wearing crosses when they took them to be killed. Also, the people who had crosses on their door were not killed. They will relate to the *tree* better than the *cross.*

    Christ has redeemed us from the curse of the law, having become a curse for us (for it is written, "*Cursed is everyone who hangs on a tree*"). (Galatians 3:13)

Christ redeemed us, Jew and Gentile, from the curse of the law by hanging on a tree and becoming that curse for us.

- Jews will also use the word *Adonai,* which is Hebrew for *Master, Lord,* or *my Lord. Redeemer* is another good word to use.

If you are serious about witnessing to Jewish people (and we should all seek opportunity to do so), study prophecies about the Messiah so you will be ready to show how Jesus fulfilled all Old Testament prophecy about the coming Redeemer. Below is a list of a few such scriptures.

Therefore the Lord Himself will give you a sign: Behold the virgin shall conceive and bear a Son, and shall call His name Immanuel. (Isaiah 7:14)

"But you, Bethlehem Ephrathah, *Though* you are little among the thousands of Judah, *Yet* out of you shall come forth to Me The One to be Ruler in Israel, Whose goings forth *are* from of old, From everlasting." (Micah 5:2)

Isaiah foretells Jesus' virgin birth and His name, and Micah prophesies in what city the birth would take place. Read the fulfillment in Matthew 1:21–23 and 2:1.

Zechariah 11:12–14 prophesies about the thirty pieces of silver and is fulfilled in Matthew 27:3–9.

Zechariah 9:9 describes in detail how Jesus would enter the city riding on a donkey—fulfilled in Matthew 21:1–9 and John 12:15.

Psalm 22:18 foretells the dividing of His garments and the casting of lots, fulfilled in Matthew 27:35.

Isaiah 53:4 says, "He was wounded for our transgressions" and "we esteemed Him stricken," fulfilled on the cross.

Psalm 69:21 foretells the vinegar Jesus was given at the cross and is confirmed in Luke 23:36, John 19:29–30, and also found in Matthew and Mark.

Zechariah 12:10 says, "They will look on Me whom they have pierced," which is fulfilled in John 19:37.

Later in this book, we will look at the book of Ruth and how beautifully it portrays redemption through Christ. Not only is this an enlightening book for Christians to read, but it is a beautiful way to share the gospel with Jewish people. On the Jewish holiday *Shavuot*, they read the book of Ruth. This is a wonderful link between their Jewish roots and Yeshua.

People are only saved by God. Some of us plant seed, some water, but only God gives the increase (1 Corinthians 3:6–7). We need to be faithful to whatever He gives us to do. We need to share Jesus with anyone who doesn't know Him—sometimes with words but more important, with our lives. We need to be good ambassadors for Christ.

The only way for anyone—Jew or Gentile—to get to heaven is to believe and accept *Yeshua, Messiah* (Jesus Christ) as Lord and Savior.

> Jesus said to him, "I am the way, the truth, and the life. No one comes to the Father except through Me." (John 14:6)

Pray for Peace in Jerusalem

Many people do not understand the importance of Israel or how much of God's Word is being fulfilled in our lifetime. The Bible is a road map of the past and of the future. Biblical prophecy always comes to pass. The prophecies about Jesus' birth, His suffering and death, were fulfilled to the letter. Countless others have been fulfilled through the ages.

The people of Israel were scattered for years. In 606 BC the Babylonian Empire destroyed most of Jerusalem. They returned in 586 BC and destroyed the Temple and scattered all the Jews. In AD 70 the Jewish Temple was destroyed and once again, the Jews were scattered without a nation. However, God brought them back. In 1948 prophecy was amazingly fulfilled when Israel once again became a nation. Astounding.

Listen to what Jesus said.

> Now as He sat on the Mount of Olives, the disciples came to Him privately, saying, "Tell us, when will these things be? And what *will be* the sign of Your coming, and of the end of the age?"

> And Jesus answered and said to them: "Take heed that no one deceives you. For many will come in My name, saying, 'I am the Christ,' and will deceive many. And you will hear of wars and rumors of wars. See that you are not troubled; for all *these things* must come to pass, but the end is not yet. For nation will rise against nation, and kingdom against kingdom. And there will be famines, pestilences, and earthquakes in various places. All these *are* the beginning of sorrows.

> "Then they will deliver you up to tribulation and kill you, and you will be hated by all nations for My name's sake. And then many will be offended, will betray one another, and will hate one another. Then many false prophets will rise up and deceive many. And because lawlessness will abound, the love of many will grow cold. But he who endures to the end shall be saved. And this gospel of the kingdom will be preached in all the world as a witness to all the nations, and then the end will come." (Matthew 24:3–14)

There have always been wars and natural disasters, but take some time to look at current statistics. You may be shocked. More severe earthquakes have been recorded in the last two decades than at any period in history. In fact, as I write this, Fox News reported a government report before the end of 2012 would show the increasing severity and the increasing trend of earthquakes within the last twenty years. Famines. Pestilences (consider AIDS). The frequency and severity of events Jesus described are multiplying at an increasingly accelerated rate never seen before.

Study the scriptures of prophecy, especially in Daniel and Revelation. Keep your eyes on Israel. We live in an exciting age as we watch prophecy after prophecy being fulfilled.

All signs suggest we are rapidly moving into the end times. Only God knows the moment Jesus will return, but He is giving us signs. Signs to get ready. This is not a time to fear—but it is a time to get busy. To share the gospel. To focus on whatever He has called us to do.

God spoke these words to Israel:

"I will bless those who bless you, And I will curse
him who curses you; And in you all the families
of the earth shall be blessed." (Genesis 12:3)

We need to bless Israel as a nation, as a church, and as
individuals. Ask God how you can do this.

He has called all of us to pray for the peace of Jerusalem
(Psalm 122:6). Everlasting or true peace will only come
when Jesus Christ, the Prince of Peace, returns to establish
His kingdom. Just as so many prophecies have been fulfilled
and more are being fulfilled each year, so will this most
exciting one of all come to pass . . .

> And while they looked steadfastly toward heaven
> as He went up, behold, two men stood by
> them in white apparel, who also said, "Men of
> Galilee, why do you stand gazing up into heaven?
> This *same* Jesus, who was taken up from you into
> heaven, will so come in like manner as you saw
> Him go into heaven." (Acts 1:10–11)

chapter 10
Islam Today

Why talk about Islam? This book is about the church and Israel.

The answer is simple: One of Islam's primary objectives is to destroy every infidel. They consider everyone who is not a Muslim an infidel. Their principal targets for destruction? Christians and Jews.

The animosity between the Muslims and the Jews goes back to Abraham's son, Ishmael. It seemed to reignite in 1948 when Israel became a nation. Muslims base their claim to the land of Israel on Ishmael. They believe the land of Canaan belongs to them. The smoldering fire began to burn when the Jews returned to Israel and their nation was reborn. Islam, which has a large following, began sending breezes and gusts of wind to fuel the rapidly spreading fire.

Origins of Islam

Allah was the chief god among numerous idols in the Kaaba—the ancient pagan temple at Mecca—and god of the local Quraish, Muhammad's tribe. Muhammad began having visitations from one he believed to be the angel Gabriel. He smashed his idols, but kept the black stone, which was set into the Kaaba's wall by Muhammad in AD 605 and is kissed today by Muslims. It is in the eastern cornerstone of the Kaaba, which is the direction to which Muslims pray. Their tradition holds that the black stone fell from heaven to show Adam and Eve where to build an altar.

Muhammad kept the name *Allah* for the god of Islam to appease his own tribe. Allah is not a father but a single entity that destroys rather than saves sinners, has no compassion on the righteous, and offers no way to redeem sinners. Most Muslims believe the only way to be saved is through strict obedience to the laws given to Muhammad.

For many (not all) Muslims, Islam teaches violence and *jihad*: to kill others and take over the world. Some Palestinian mothers on the border of Israel teach their children to hate, sending them to throw stones at the Israeli guards. If a child is killed doing this, the parents say that he died for Allah and will go to Paradise.

Muslim Beliefs

Islam is the fastest-growing religion in the world. Muslims' stated goal is to convert the world to Islam. If a person does not convert, Islamic teachings direct Muslims to kill the infidel or subject him to pay a special tax and rule over him.

Muslims believe the entire world should abide by sharia

law. Some Muslims believe that someday sharia will be international law.

> Sharia is the body of Islamic law implemented in Muslim countries across the world including Libya and Sudan, although most modern Islamic nations operate a dual legal system with elements of secular law alongside it. All aspects of a Muslim's life are governed by sharia, which is derived from a combination of sources including the Koran, the Hadith—the sayings and conduct of the prophet Muhammad—and fatwas, the rulings of Islamic scholars.[17]

> Under Muslim Sharia law, the clothes you wear, the music you listen to, and the television you watch would all be censored. Behavior in public is legally restricted and controlled. And Sharia is the ideal social system for those that preach Radical Islam. Sharia is an Arabic term referring to a legal framework to regulate public and private aspects of life based upon specific Islamic teachings. Sharia is an intolerant system that threatens the Western ideals of "liberty and justice for all." Sharia views non-Muslims as second class citizens, sanctions inequality between men and women, prescribes cruel and unusual punishments for crimes, and promotes a restrictive business environment that strangles the freedoms of capitalism.[18]

Muslims do not believe Jesus is God. Their salvation is based on accepting the words of Muhammad and obeying everything he said. Salvation comes through works. Many do not believe they can know where they will spend eternity.

Some Muslims believe that to die killing infidels automatically earns them immense blessings in Paradise.

The Qur'an, purportedly dictated to Muhammad, contradicts the Bible in many areas, including the fact that Jesus died and rose again. It does include some variations of biblical history—but with many differences.

> In the seventh century, Muhammad claimed the angel Gabriel visited him. During these angelic visitations, which continued for about 23 years until Muhammad's death, the angel purportedly revealed to Muhammad the words of Allah (the Arabic word for "God" used by Muslims). These dictated revelations compose the Qur'an, Islam's holy book.[19]

Many Muslims also consider that Jews and Christians have corrupted the Bible and that only their Qur'an is true. Some Muslims who read the Bible to prove it is corrupted have accepted Jesus as their Savior as the truth of God's Word changes their heart.

> Having outlined just a handful of many problems and difficulties pertaining to the Qur'an as a divinely inspired work, we are all but forced to reject the Islamic claim that the Qur'an represents an error-free word of God to humanity. When a similar standard is applied to the Bible, the result is self-vindicating, for the Bible emerges flawless.[20]

Consumed with a Passion to Destroy

President Mahmoud Ahmadinejad of Iran believes that a war with Israel will please Allah, his god. He has told the world he is making nuclear materials to provide energy needs for his country. The world knows this same material can be used to destroy their enemy. It seems to be clear that they consider Israel their enemy number one and the United States number two.

> Today, most prophecy-watchers are on high alert. Israel is threatened by enemies on all sides. The Muslim Brotherhood has taken control of entire countries, seemingly overnight. Iranian madman, Mahmoud Ahmadinejad, calls for Israel's complete destruction. Vladimir Putin cozies up to Syria and their increasingly desperate despot, who still clings to power. Enemies and massive weaponry are everywhere—Palestinians, Hezbollah, Hamas ... bombs, missiles and rockets ... how much longer can it be before we have a deadly nuclear confrontation?[21]

Satan must be happy with all the false teachings that bring people down to his pits. He should be in unusually high spirits with the Islamic religion because they have something in common: Satan tried to wipe the Jews off the earth when Haman, an enemy of the Jews, tried to destroy them (Esther 7:5–6). He tried again beginning in 1938 through Hitler, who tried to destroy all the Jews. Ahmadinejad and Islam militants now want to destroy them.

Appeasement and tolerance did not work in 1938 with

Hitler. They will never work when a tyrant wants power. They will never work when they are consumed with such passion.

†

Sharing Jesus with Muslims

We must remember that not all Muslims are militant and Christ died for everyone, including the militants. We all came into this world as sinners.

We should communicate to the Palestinians and all Muslims the truths of the Bible and help them understand that Jesus is their Savior. Many know about Jesus, and that is a good talking point with which to begin. They do not believe Jesus is God. Pray as you witness. Stay strong in your Christian beliefs.

Here is the story that needs to be told to the world: Jesus created this world and everybody in it. He came to earth and was the only person to live a sinless life. While on earth, He was all God and all man. He was rejected because not only did the people not believe, but they also lied and told false stories to convict Him. They prodded the Romans to kill Him. In reality, Jesus set the time and the place and allowed them to kill Him. He suffered the worst death anybody could suffer.

Jesus created the mountain where they crucified Him. He created the timber for the cross and the metal for the nails. They stripped His clothes and let Him hang naked, humiliated, in front of His mother and His friends. He died for everybody, but sadly, most will reject Him. The only way to heaven is to believe and accept Jesus Christ as our Savior (Titus 1:4). We have only one God and in that one God are the Father, Son, and Holy Spirit. Christianity is exclusive; it is based on our relationship with Jesus Christ (John 14:6; Romans 1:16; 3:23; 5:8; 6:23; 10:9–10; 10:13; 1 Corinthians 15:1–4).

> Who is a liar but he who denies that Jesus is the Christ? He is antichrist who denies the Father and the Son. (1 John 2:22)

According to the above scripture, anyone who denies that Jesus Christ is God is lying. The Scriptures state that Satan is a liar and a deceiver. (Other verses to read along this line are Matthew 24:5; Mark 13:6; Romans 16:18; Ephesians 5:6; 2 Thessalonians 2:3; and Jude 1:19.)

> "Do not fear those who kill the body but cannot kill the soul. But rather fear Him who is able to destroy both soul and body in hell." (Matthew 10:28)

chapter 11

Still to Come

Studying God's Word is like putting a puzzle together. Placing one piece in the right location can open your eyes to see where the other pieces of the puzzle go. You can see more of the picture.

The more we understand God's plan, the more He will open our eyes and our hearts. The truths revealed in the book of Revelation are an essential part of the puzzle. Other parts of the Bible that help complete the picture include the Old Testament, Jesus' teaching in the gospels, and especially the writings of Paul teaching truths revealed to him by Jesus Christ for us in this age of grace.

The book of Revelation is a revelation of Jesus Christ and discloses much of our future. It also correlates the prophecies in the Old Testament with those in the New Testament, helping the puzzle come together. Revelation is the only book in the Bible that tells us we will be blessed if we read or hear its words.

> Blessed *is* he who reads and those who hear the
> words of this prophecy, and keeps those things

which are written in it; for the time *is* near.
(Revelation 1:3)

Jesus Will Come for the Church: The Rapture

Jesus revealed several mysteries to Paul. One of those mysteries discloses a time when all believers (both Jews and Gentiles) will be "caught up" in the air: the rapture (see 1 Thessalonians 4:13–18). Scriptures clearly say Jesus will come down from the heavens and call His believers, the church, to Him. With this special event, the age of grace and the times of the Gentiles will end.

> For the Lord Himself will descend from heaven with a shout, with the voice of an archangel, and with the trumpet of God. And the dead in Christ will rise first. Then we who are alive *and* remain shall be caught up together with them in the clouds to meet the Lord in the air. (1 Thessalonians 4:16–17)

After all the believers are caught up in the rapture, the world will be left on a course to its destined doom: days of wrath never before seen.

Ken Johnson, in his book *Ancient Prophecies Revealed,* writes this:

> The church age ends with the Laodecian church being so liberal/ lukewarm that they no longer seriously believe in the pre-tribulation Rapture. They are not looking for it and it catches them off guard (Luke 17:26–36).

> The Rapture of believers may not be much of a shock if shortly after the Rapture takes place, one quarter of the world's population dies in various events: earthquake, famine, plague, etc. They may simply assume those Raptured were killed in some similar catastrophe. Those who lost their first love will not be looking for Jesus to Rapture them but look for the church to conquer. At the First Coming, the Jews wanted a Messiah to rule and reign so they *spiritualized* the prophecies of the suffering Messiah. Before the Second Coming, the church will *spiritualize* the Tribulation and Millennial reign because they want to be the ones who take over the earth.[22]

When the church is gone, God will once again turn His focus to His people, Israel, and fulfill His covenants with them. Daniel's vision and prophecies about Judah and Jerusalem will be largely fulfilled during this time. Many will be saved (mostly Jews) and the Jewish people will share the good news with others. See Revelation chapter seven.

The word *rapture* is found in the Latin Bible. English Bibles translate it as "snatching away." In Greek, the word is *harpazo,* but in the Latin it is *raptus.* It is translated in English as "caught up" (see 1Thessalonians 4:17). Scriptures about the rapture, being caught up, remind us of at least three truths.

1. Believers in Christ, while on this earth, are waiting to receive new bodies immediately after the people in heaven receive their new bodies. Jesus Christ is with us who belong to Him now. He will never leave us!

At the rapture, He will take us with Him, and we will receive new bodies!

"Behold, I tell you a mystery: We shall not all sleep, but we shall all be changed—in a moment, in the twinkling of an eye, at the last trumpet." (1 Corinthians 15:51–52)

For our citizenship is in heaven, from which we also eagerly wait for the Savior, the Lord Jesus Christ, who will transform our lowly body that it may be conformed to His glorious body, according to the working by which He is able even to subdue all things to Himself. (Philippians 3:20–21)

2. God created our souls to live forever. Jesus Christ has taken away our sins and has made us blameless.

    God gave us the breath of life. That makes humans distinct from all other creatures. He gave us soul and spirit to live forever.

    And the LORD God formed man *of* the dust of the ground, and breathed into his nostrils the breath of life; and man became a living being. (Genesis 2:7)

    Then the dust will return to the earth as it was, And the spirit will return to God who gave it. (Ecclesiastes 12:7)

    Although we have all sinned, if we receive Jesus as Lord and Savior, He takes away our sins and makes us blameless. We pass from death to life.

"I tell you the truth, whoever hears my word and believes him who sent me has eternal life and will not be condemned; he has crossed over from death to life." (John 5:24 NIV)

3. The other significant issue in 1 Thessalonians 4:17 is that Jesus Christ will take us with Him. More importantly, we will always be with Him!

Now this is powerful! The Lord Himself will come back for His believers. This could be soon!

During the rapture, the generation of born-again Christians still on this earth will be gone in a moment. In the Greek, a moment is the shortest divisible portion of time, less than a second.

Paul wrote this exciting description of what is to come.

Behold, I tell you a mystery: We shall not all sleep, but we shall all be changed—in a moment, in the twinkling of an eye, at the last trumpet. For the trumpet will sound, and the dead will be raised incorruptible, and we shall be changed. For this corruptible must put on incorruption, and this mortal *must* put on immortality. So when this corruptible has put on incorruption, and this mortal has put on immortality, then shall be brought to pass the saying that is written: "*Death is swallowed up in victory.*" (1 Corinthians 15:51–54)

In a moment, our souls—if we are believers—will leave our bodies and be with Christ before we can blink an eye.

In the Old Testament, God told His people to bring their firstfruits to the Lord—the first of the grain, the first of the harvest. Scripture tells us Christ became the firstfruits of all who had died. He was the first to rise from the dead. To be bodily transformed. And someday every believer will be resurrected.

> But now Christ is risen from the dead *and* has become the firstfruits of those who have fallen asleep. (1 Corinthians 15:20)

After Jesus Christ was resurrected, graves opened and many saints were resurrected (Matthew 27:52). People witnessed those who were once dead walking around town. Sown in corruption, people were raised in incorruption.

> So also *is* the resurrection of the dead. *The body* is sown in corruption, it is raised in incorruption. It is sown in dishonor, it is raised in glory. It is sown in weakness, it is raised in power. It is sown a natural body, it is raised a spiritual body. There is a natural body, and there is a spiritual body. (1Corinthians 15:42–44)

Our earthly bodies will be planted in the ground, buried in brokenness—but they will be raised in glory. Our present body is perishable and prone to decay, but our spiritual body will never get sick and will not be limited by the laws of nature. The Scriptures tell us our new body will be like Jesus' body!

> For our citizenship is in heaven, from which we also eagerly wait for the Savior, the Lord Jesus Christ, who will transform our lowly body that it may be conformed to His glorious body,

according to the working by which He is able even to subdue all things to Himself. (Philippians 3:20–21)

Paul wrote most of the verses about the rapture, but Jesus talked about it too. In the following passage, Jesus was talking to Martha, the sister of Lazarus, who was in the grave. He encouraged her with these words of hope:

> Jesus said to her, "I am the resurrection and the life. He who believes in Me, though he may die, he shall live. And whoever lives and believes in Me shall never die. Do you believe this?" (John 11:25–26)

The Rapture: Before, During, or After the Tribulation?

Believers differ about when the rapture will take place. There are three schools of thought: before the tribulation (pre-tribulation), halfway through the tribulation (mid-tribulation), and after the tribulation (post-tribulation).

I have studied all viewpoints, and I believe the Scriptures strongly suggest the rapture will take place before the tribulation. Christ will take us, the church, from this earth before the tribulation begins.

> God has now revealed to us his mysterious plan about Christ, a plan to fulfill his own good pleasure. And this is the plan: At the right time he will bring everything together under the authority of Christ—everything in heaven and on earth. (Ephesians 1:9–10 NLT)

God has a perfect plan—and a perfect timetable for that plan. The church and Israel are two distinct groups, and God has a separate plan for each. Everyone in both groups is a sinner and needs salvation. People in both groups can be saved only by receiving Jesus Christ as Lord and Savior. Everyone who receives Jesus is forgiven of their sins and will spend eternity in heaven. However, the history for the two groups is very different. And their paths through the end times are not the same.

Throughout the Old Testament, from the time of Abraham, God's focus was on the Hebrew people, Israel. In the New Testament before Pentecost there were followers of Christ—His disciples and many others. But there was no church—they were a part of spiritual Israel. After Pentecost, the church was born, but spiritual Israel faded away. Because Israel rejected the Messiah at His first coming, the time of the Gentiles came in and the church age began. After the rapture, there will be no church, but a spiritual Israel will come into prominence again. The true believers with faith in Christ (both Jew and Gentile) will be raptured. Unbelievers who claim to be part of the church but never received Christ and all unbelievers (both Jew and Gentile) will be left behind and experience the Great Tribulation.

The Great Tribulation

Scriptures tell us the Great Tribulation will bring wrath and chaos greater than the world has ever seen. Prophecies about this time appear in Isaiah 34, Revelation, Daniel, Jeremiah, Zechariah, and many other books in the Bible.

Paul talks about the mystery in Ephesians 3: Jesus will come for His saints and remove them from this earth. But will this happen before the Great Tribulation?

In Philippians 3:20–21, Paul says we should look eagerly for our Savior. People who believe in mid- or post-tribulation will look forward to this time with dread. They will focus on the tribulation, the Antichrist, and a taste of God's wrath—instead of fervently watching for Jesus Christ.

God did not "appoint us to wrath."

> For God did not appoint us to wrath, but to obtain salvation through our Lord Jesus Christ, who died for us, that whether we wake or sleep, we should live together with Him. Therefore comfort each other and edify one another, just as you also are doing. (1 Thessalonians 5:9–11)

God chose to save us through our Lord Jesus Christ, not to punish or pour out His anger on us. Several more scriptures talk about saving us from His wrath. God's punishment is far worse than any punishment the devil can give out.

Consider this: Don't you think while Paul was writing to the churches and warning them about persecution that he would have told them about the Great Tribulation if believers were going to go through it?

Paul does not usually talk about prophecy, but in his second recorded letter to the Thessalonians, he addresses the future to put the new believers at ease. They feared they had missed the rapture and were in the Great Tribulation.

> And to *give* you who are troubled rest with us

> when the Lord Jesus is revealed from heaven with
> His mighty angels. (2 Thessalonians 1:7)

Paul assured them they would be spared from God's wrath in the Day of the Lord, which he refers to as "the day of Christ."

> Now, brethren, concerning the coming of our
> Lord Jesus Christ and our gathering together to
> Him, we ask you, not to be soon shaken in mind
> or troubled, either by spirit or by word or by
> letter, as if from us, as though the day of Christ
> had come. (2 Thessalonians 2:1–3)

> Note in NKJV: "The Greek word translated
> **gathering together** is found in the NT only here
> and in Hebrews 10:25. There it refers to the local
> congregation, while here it is the congregation of
> the whole church. This will be the first time the
> whole church, including every believer, will be
> gathered before the Lord to worship Him."

The subject is the pre-tribulation rapture of the church. Let's examine Paul's words.

> Then we who are alive *and* remain shall be caught
> up together with them in the clouds to meet the
> Lord in the air. And thus we shall always be with
> the Lord. (1 Thessalonians 4:17)

Paul uses the pronoun *we*, including himself. In the next chapter where he is talking about the day of the Lord, he uses the pronoun *they*.

For when they say, "Peace and safety!" then sudden destruction comes upon them. (1 Thessalonians 5:3)

Paul does not include himself when he is talking about the wrath experienced in the Day of the Lord. Those familiar with Hebrew Scriptures would know this is a reference to a time of darkness and judgment against sinful people,

Let no one deceive you by any means; for *that Day will not come* unless the falling away comes first, and the man of sin is revealed, the son of perdition. (2 Thessalonians 2:3)

In this verse, the term *falling away* has two sides to it. Some Bible scholars state *falling away* means "departure" in older writings. This would mean believers would be gone before the Great Tribulation. Others state that *falling away* means the churches will fall away from Christ. Both of these definitions ring true.

Paul talks about the "son of perdition." There is little doubt that this is the Antichrist, and he will be filled with evil from Satan.

For the mystery of lawlessness is already at work; only He who now restrains *will do so* until He is taken out of the way. (2 Thessalonians 2:7)

The word *until* is referring to the rapture —and only God knows when that time will come. The Holy Spirit will restrain evil until then. Once the believers are removed, the flood of evil will pour in. It will be like a dam breaking, spilling a great flood of evil and wickedness on the world.

At this point, believers will already be in heaven waiting to return with Christ. *Ten thousands* is a Hebrew expression meaning a limitless number. When the rapture occurs, Christ will come *for* His saints (1 Thessalonians 4:15–18), and later He will return *with* His saints (1 Thessalonians 3:13; Jude 1:14; Revelation 19:14) to set up His kingdom on earth.

True believers will face Jesus at the judgment seat to receive rewards.

> Therefore we make it our aim, whether present or absent, to be well pleasing to Him. For we must all appear before the judgment seat of Christ, that each one may receive the things *done* in the body, according to what he has done, whether good or bad. (2 Corinthians 5:9–10)

This could sound frightening at first reading, but after looking into this and seeing the love our Lord has for us, I realized it is not to be feared. From everything I read and study, this will take place in heaven shortly after the rapture. I think it will be one-on-one. We will be aware of what we did on earth, both good and bad.

This judgment seat is called the *Bema seat,* referring to a raised platform where judges give out rewards and crowns to the winners of athletic events. The thought that each one of us must give an account of our lives before the omniscient and Holy God should be a reminder to us as we direct our thoughts to heaven and to Jesus Christ. We will stand before

Christ and account for everything we have done on this earth.

> But I do not want you to be ignorant, brethren, concerning those who have fallen asleep, lest you sorrow as others who have no hope. For if we believe that Jesus died and rose again, even so God will bring with Him those who sleep in Jesus. For this we say to you by the word of the Lord, that we who are alive *and* remain until the coming of the Lord will by no means precede those who are asleep. For the Lord Himself will descend from heaven with a shout, with the voice of an archangel, and with the trumpet of God. And the dead in Christ will rise first. Then we who are alive *and* remain shall be caught up together with them in the clouds to meet the Lord in the air. And thus we shall always be with the Lord. Therefore comfort one another with these words. (1 Thessalonians 4:13–18)

I hope these scriptures will comfort you and help you anticipate His coming with joy. Titus 2:13 tells us to look for "the blessed hope and glorious appearing of our great God and Savior Jesus Christ."

After the Rapture

After the rapture, all the believers will be gone from the earth and celebrating in heaven with Jesus Christ. The next season on earth will begin with only unbelievers. God will then turn His attention to Israel and get ready for the seventieth week described by Daniel. He prophesied about the evil one: "Then he shall confirm a covenant with many for one week" (Daniel 9:27). John called him an antichrist: "This is a deceiver and an antichrist" (2 John 1:7). Bible scholars think that with the rise of the Antichrist, the Great Tribulation will begin. He will confirm a seven-year treaty of peace with Israel—a treaty he will break after three and one-half years.

In that day, Israel will be living under the law as it was in the Old Testament. Midway through the seven years, the Antichrist will defile the Temple. "But in the middle of the week he shall bring an end to sacrifice and offering" (Daniel 9:27).

That will be a disastrous time. Jesus said this about the tribulation: "And pray that your flight may not be in winter or on the Sabbath" (Matthew 24:20). The good news is that many people, largely led by Jewish people who will become believers after the rapture, will receive Jesus Christ as Lord and Savior during the tribulation. The bad news is that many won't.

Millennium

What will happen at the end of the seven years of tribulation? Jesus tells us here.

> "Immediately after the tribulation of those days the sun will be darkened, and the moon will not give its light; the stars will fall from heaven, and the powers of the heavens will be shaken. Then the sign of the Son of Man will appear in heaven, and then all the tribes of the earth will mourn,

and they will see the Son of Man coming on the clouds of heaven with power and great glory. And He will send His angels with a great sound of a trumpet, and they will gather together His elect from the four winds, from one end of heaven to the other." (Matthew 24:29–31)

Jesus will return to earth to set up His kingdom. He will come on a white horse and will bring with Him the armies of heaven (Revelation 19:14) and His saints (Jude 1:14). I can picture us sailing from the third heaven through the stars and universe to the earth! What a view we will have! Jesus Christ knows how He will bring us back; I know it will be wonderful. The Scriptures tell us that we will have new glorified bodies. What I glean from this is that we will be the heavenly people, and we will be with Jesus Christ when He rules the earthly people in His kingdom.

In Matthew 25:31–46 we learn that Jesus will cleanse the earth of all sinful people to make way for the New Millennium. He will defeat the Antichrist and all his evil in the Battle of Armageddon. And then He will divide the goats from the sheep.

People of faith will experience eternal life with God. The goats, the unbelievers, have never exercised faith. They have done evil and refused to believe in Christ—now they are forever condemned. Unlike the believers, they will not be spending eternity with Jesus—they will suffer an eternity of hell.

And I saw the dead, small and great, standing before God, and books were opened. And another

> book was opened, which is *the Book* of Life. And
> the dead were judged according to their works,
> by the things which were written in the books.
> (Revelation 20:12)

Notice the *Book of Life* is singular, but the *books,* plural. These books contain the account of the lost, who will be judged. Nobody can escape. What will happen to them?

> "And anyone not found written in the Book of
> Life was cast into the lake of fire." (Revelation
> 20:15)

We don't like to read this, but it is the Word of God. When Jesus was on earth, He said it this way.

> "Therefore as the tares are gathered and burned
> in the fire, so it will be at the end of this age. The
> Son of Man will send out His angels, and they
> will gather out of His kingdom all things that
> offend, and those who practice lawlessness, and
> will cast them into the furnace of fire. There
> will be wailing and gnashing of teeth. Then
> the righteous will shine forth as the sun in the
> kingdom of their Father. He who has ears to hear,
> let him hear!" (Matthew 13:40–43)

Is your name in the Book of Life? Will you be with Jesus Christ forever? Are you ready?

chapter 12

Are You Ready?

Redeem. Webster's defines it as "to buy back: repurchase; to get or win back; to free from captivity by payment or ransom."

The book of Ruth is a story about a redeemer. It starts with a woman named Naomi. This woman was among the poorest people in Israel. However, one of her relatives, Boaz, was among the richest men in Israel. Naomi and her family had gone to live in a foreign land because of a severe famine in Israel. Her husband and her two sons died there. She eventually went back to her homeland with her daughter-in-law Ruth, who was a Gentile from the country of Moab. When they arrived in Israel, they had no means of support. By law, Ruth could glean grain from the neighbors' fields. The field she chose belonged to Boaz.

Unknown to Ruth, Boaz was a distant relative of her husband, who had passed away. Raised as a Gentile, she had no idea what that could mean to her future. In Israel, the nearest relative, or kinsman, had the right to redeem (purchase) Naomi's property and marry Ruth. Their first son would belong to Ruth's dead husband and continue his name through a line of descendants. Naomi's nearest of kin decided not to redeem the property when he learned there was a young widow involved. That left Boaz, the next closest kinsman, to redeem the land and marry Ruth.

A *kinsman redeemer* was a relative who could redeem or buy back. The requirements to be a kinsman redeemer included these:

- Must be a kinsman (Leviticus 25:47–49; Ruth 3:12–13)
- Must be able to perform the redemption (Ruth 4:4–6)
- Must be willing (Ruth 4:6)
- Must assume the entire obligation (Leviticus 25:24–27; Ruth 4:7–11)

Boaz had to meet these requirements to acquire Naomi's property and marry Ruth. He had to check the records and find out whether the next of kin was willing to perform the redemption and then be next in line to meet the kinsman responsibility. The other requirement was that he be able to perform the duties of the kinsman. He also needed to be willing to assume the entire obligation (Ruth 4:1–12). Boaz fulfilled that obligation and married Ruth. King David is their great-grandson. A much later descendant would be the true Redeemer, Jesus Christ.

> In whom we have Redemption through His blood, the forgiveness of sins. (Colossians 1:14)

We All Need a Redeemer

God created a perfect man and woman: Adam and Eve. And He placed them in a perfect place, the garden of Eden. God gave them dominion over all creation.

Everything in the garden was for Adam and Eve's pleasure—except one tree. The Tree of Knowledge of Good and Evil. "God has said, You shall not eat it, nor shall you touch it, lest you die" (Genesis 3:3). God gave Adam a choice. To obey—or not.

Adam made a bad choice. He disobeyed God and sin entered the world.

God is a holy God and there can be no sin in His presence. Before Adam and Eve's disobedience, God had walked and talked with them in the garden. But now sin separated them. The final consequence of sin is death.

Adam and Eve needed to be restored to fellowship. And because of what they had done, everyone born since then has been born with a sinful nature. We are all captive to sin and need to be "set free from captivity by payment or ransom." We need to be redeemed. Bought back with a price.

Jesus paid that price.

> Therefore, just as through one man sin entered the world, and death through sin, and thus death spread to all men, because all sinned . . . (For if by the one man's offense death reigned through the one, much more those who receive abundance of grace and of the gift of righteousness will reign in life through the One, Jesus Christ.) Therefore, as through one man's offense *judgment came* to all men, resulting in condemnation, even so through

one Man's righteous act *the free gift came* to all men, resulting in justification of life. For as by one man's disobedience many were made sinners, so also by one Man's obedience many will be made righteous. (Romans 5:12, 17–19)

Adam needed a kinsman redeemer—and so does every person who has ever lived. You do. And I do. A much-sung hymn says it this way:

He paid a debt He did not owe
I owed a debt I could not pay.[23]

The debt? Sin.

For all have sinned and fall short of the glory of God. (Romans 3:23)

Payment we owe? Death.

For the wages of sin *is* death. (Romans 6:23)

Jesus, who was without sin and owed no debt, paid our debt for us.

For God made Christ, who never sinned, to be the offering for our sin, so that we could be made right with God through Christ. (2 Corinthians 5:21 NLT)

While He was dying on the cross, Jesus cried out the Greek word *Tetelestai,* which means, "It is finished!"

In New Testament times, when a person paid off the obligation of a debt, they often wrote *Tetelestai* on the note or document, declaring the debt was paid in full, finished. This was a word people understood in those days. I have read that after a person paid off his land or debt, he would run up the street waving his debt release paper, crying out, *Tetelestai, Tetelestai.* It is finished!

Jesus was declaring the job was done. He was our redeemer—ready, and able, and willing to fulfill the entire obligation. He paid for our sins in full.

What Is Next?

So is that it? Everyone is saved from sin and will go to heaven because Jesus has paid the price? No.

Jesus has paid the price. He offers everyone forgiveness as a gift. But we must believe He is the Son of God and paid the price for our sin. We must reach out and accept that gift. And if we truly believe, we will invite Him to be Lord of our life.

> If you confess with your mouth that Jesus is Lord and believe in your heart that God raised him from the dead, you will be saved. For it is by believing in your heart that you are made right with God, and it is by confessing with your mouth that you are saved. As the Scriptures tell us, "Anyone who trusts in him will never be disgraced." Jew and Gentile are the same in this respect. They have the same Lord, who gives generously to all who call on him. For "Everyone who calls on the name of the LORD will be saved." (Romans 10:9–13 NLT)

Is There Any Other Way?

In a word, no.

Some think if they live a good life, they will go to heaven. They will earn their way. But this is what the Bible says:

> God saved you by his grace when you believed. And you can't take credit for this; it is a gift from God. Salvation is not a reward for the good things we have done, so none of us can boast about it. (Ephesians 2:8–9 NLT)

> But—"When God our Savior revealed his kindness and love, he saved us, not because of the righteous things we had done, but because of his mercy. He washed away our sins, giving us a new birth and new life through the Holy Spirit." (Titus 3:4–5 NLT)

And some think as long as you sincerely believe something—whatever it is—you will be saved. But Jesus clearly said He is the only way.

> Jesus told him, "I am the way, the truth, and the life. No one can come to the Father except through me." (John 14:6 NLT)

Why Did God Do This?

You may ask why a perfect God would even care about us. Since we have all sinned, why not allow us to get what we deserve? Why would He send His only son to earth to suffer and die?

Love. Amazingly, though we do not deserve it, He loves us that much.

> God showed how much he loved us by sending his one and only Son into the world so that we might have eternal life through him. This is real love—not that we loved God, but that he loved us and sent his Son as a sacrifice to take away our sins. (1 John 4:9–10 NLT)

How About You? Are You Ready?

Are you ready to die? Do you know you will spend eternity with Jesus? If you have received Him as your Lord and Savior, you are ready. If not, are you ready to do that now?

God loves you. Jesus paid the price for your sins. Are you ready to receive His gift . . . and follow Him? Receiving Jesus doesn't mean all your problems on this earth will vanish. But it does mean you will not have to face them alone.

If you are ready to choose Jesus, just tell Him. Right now. Admit you are a sinner. Admit that you need Him and want Him in your life. No matter what you may have done . . . He is waiting for you . . .

Into the Arms of Jesus

My wife Jeannette had been in bed for five days with a body full of cancer, waiting to die. She always had a smile on her face and a laugh in her heart. She was sharing her love for

Christ with everybody who came into her room. People were coming and going from morning to night.

After about five days, Jeannette said to me, "I have not had much time with you. Will you lie down with me?" My daughters stepped outside the room and closed the door behind them. I pulled back the covers and crawled under the tubes and life support connected to her and in her. I slid my left arm under her head and held the tubes from coming out with the other hand. Before we could start a conversation, she went into a deep sleep.

Soon after that, she went from a steady low breathing to deep breathing. She seemed to be struggling to get enough air to stay alive. Then she called out in a normal voice, "Jesus." Her breathing became short and not as deep. A second time she called out, "Jesus."

I was sure she was dying and going into the arms of Jesus. I thought it would be selfish not to share this with my daughters, who were waiting outside the door. I came out from under the sheet and the medical tubes and with my loud voice said, "Come in here. Your mother is dying and going to heaven." They immediately rushed in. My wife's breathing went back to normal. It was the next day before she went to heaven.

I related the story to the woman who owned the hospice house. She stated she had seen similar times when it appeared people were dying. Some had smiles on their face or were talking about a beautiful place. People in the room would start singing or talking, and the departing person refocused on his or her surroundings and was distracted from the heavenlies. This would delay death for a day or more. She agreed with me. If I had not moved out of bed so fast with a loud yell, most likely she would have gone from my arms into the arms of Jesus Christ.

How about you? When your time comes, will you move . . . into the arms of Jesus?

Endnotes

1. J. Dwight Pentecost. *Things to Come* (Grand Rapids, MI: Zondervan Publishing House, reprint 1964), 75.

2. Daniel March (1816-1909), *Night Scenes in the Bible* (Philadelphia: Zeigler & McCurdy), 286–287.

3. March, *Night Scenes in the Bible*, 292–293.

4. Ken Johnson, *Ancient Prophecies Revealed: 500 Prophecies Listed in Order of When They Were Fulfilled.* (2008), 38.

5. *The Works of Flavius Josephus*, tr. William Whiston, commentary by Paul L. Maier (Grand Rapids, Mich.: Kregel Publications, 1999), 886–889.

6. William Koenig, *Eye to Eye: Facing the Consequences of Dividing Israel* (Alexandria, Vir.: About Him Publishers, 2007), 135–136.

7. Koenig, *Eye to Eye*, 177–178.

8. Koenig, *Eye to Eye*, 177–178.

9. "About Us." *Ministry to Israel:* http://ministrytoisrael.com/about-us/ (January 24, 2013).

10. Les Feldick, *Through the Bible with Les Feldick,* audio cassette (Kinta, Okla: Les Feldick Ministries, 2001).

11. Pentecost, *Things to Come,* 453.

12. William R. Newell, Bible Student's Notebook. *www. BibleStudentsNotebook.com.*

13. Ronald Youngblood, F.F. Bruce, and R.K. Harrison.

The Nelson's Student Bible Dictionary: A Complete Guide to Understanding the Word of the Bible (Nashville, Tenn: Thomas Nelson, Inc., 2005), 317–318.

14. "Part 6: Faith 'Tribes,'" *State of the Church Series, 2011,* August 4, 2011. *Barna Group: http://www.barna.org/faith-spirituality/514-barna-study-of-religious-change-since-1991-shows-significant-changes-by-faith-group?q=faith+commitment* (February 19, 2013).

15. Matt Slick, "What Is the New Age Movement," *Religious Groups and Cults. CARM: http://carm.org/new-age-what* (February 19, 2013).

16. Steve Ertelt, "Abortion Has Destroyed 117 Million People in the United States." *LifeNews.com: http://www.lifenews. com/2012/11/06/abortion-has-destroyed-117-million-people-in-the-united-states* (February 19, 2013).

17. "what is sharia law?" News: UK News. *Telegraph:* http://www.telegraph.co.uk/news/uknews/1578018/What–is–sharia–law.html (February 27, 2013).

18. "Sharia Law." *RadicalIslam.org:* http://www.radicalislam.org/threat/global–threat/sharia–law (February 27, 2013).

19. "What is Islam, and what do Muslims Believe?" *GotQuestions?org:* http://www.gotquestions.org/Islam.html (February 27, 2013).

20. "Are there errors in the Qur'an (Koran)? *GotQuestions?org:* http://www.gotquestions.org/errors–Quran.html (February 27, 2013).

21. Bob Ulrich, "Bob Reviews Psalm 83 Book DVD." February 28, 2013. *Prophecy in the News: http://* www.prophecyinthenews.com (March 2013).

22. Johnson, *Ancient Prophecies Revealed, 140.*

23. Ellis J. Crum, "He Paid a Debt He Did Not Know," Ellis J. Crum, 1982.

About the Author

I grew up on a small cotton farm in West Texas near a town called Munday. When I was twelve, our preacher took my brother and me to a three-day Baptist camp. There I acknowledged Jesus Christ as my Savior.

We moved to Dallas when I was thirteen and immediately needed money, so I started delivering *The Dallas Morning News*. On my paper route, I met a girl named Jeannette. I married her eleven days after turning seventeen—she was sixteen.

After serving in the Navy, I earned my degree in business, and Jeannette received her degree in art. She died of breast cancer, February 2009. After her death, I wanted to know everything I could about the place she was in and began searching the Bible to learn about heaven.

Jeannette and I were married almost 55 years and had three daughters, nine grandchildren, and seven great grandchildren.

In April 2010, I met Judy, who had lost her husband after a long illness, and we married in 2011. Judy is my prayer partner, and she supports me as I endeavor to share the good news of Jesus Christ.

We live in Phoenix, Arizona in the winter and travel to Whidbey Island, Washington, for the summers. Together we have five children, fourteen grandchildren, and eleven great grandchildren.

Author's Statement

> For whatever things were written before were written for our learning, that we through the patience and comfort of the Scriptures might have hope (Romans 15:4).

Talking with many people who attend church regularly, I realized that many did not know—or were misinformed— about Israel. Then a person gave my daughter a book claiming the church has replaced Israel. The Scriptures were being misinterpreted. I think that was God's way of introducing me to what is called *Replacement Theology*. It was during this time I felt God wanted me to continue in His Word with study and research. I also believe He was giving me a message to share with others.

> Not that we are sufficient of ourselves to think of anything as *being* from ourselves, but our sufficiency *is* from God. (2 Corinthians 2:5).

I pray and trust that God will use this message to open people's eyes more fully to the truths in His Word and help them receive the many blessings just waiting for them. And I hope readers will better understand the importance of

Israel and the time we live in now. With God, we can have peace while looking forward to the return of Jesus Christ, our Savior.

> May God bless you and may
> His Scriptures indwell you!